# The Divine Risk

# The Divine Risk

*Introduced and edited by*
Richard Holloway

Darton, Longman and Todd
London

First published in 1990 by
Darton, Longman and Todd Ltd
89 Lillie Road, London SW6 1UD

**British Library Cataloguing in Publication Data**
The Divine risk.
1. Theology
I. Holloway, Richard, *1933–*
230

ISBN 0–232–51881–5

Phototypeset by Input Typesetting Ltd, London
Printed and bound in Great Britain by
Courier International Ltd, Tiptree, Essex

To
Philip Crosfield

# Contents

# Preface

This book of essays had a complicated origin. During Advent 1986 I delivered a series of lectures at St Mary's Cathedral, Edinburgh, on the seven gifts of the Holy Spirit, one of which is the gift of courage or fortitude. I pointed out that courage was really the basis of all the other virtues and without it the virtuous life was hardly possible at all. Nevertheless, it is a difficult and frightening gift either to seek or to cultivate, and most Christians settle for a quiet life in which courage is rarely needed. This is perhaps the most vivid contrast between us and our Lord. Courage and faith were his most conspicuous characteristics and his call to us to risk all for the sake of the kingdom is a challenge that makes most of us shiver with apprehension.

Some time after that lecture I was approached by Dr Brian Kilbey, a scientist at Edinburgh University, and the Reverend John Clarke, who was then Information and Communications Officer of the Scottish Episcopal Church. Brian Kilbey was intrigued by the whole idea of courage and risk-taking and felt that we ought to explore it further in a more deeply theological way. He felt, quite rightly, that the idea of risk was an essential part of the Christian understanding of God and wondered if it might not be possible to explore the concept of divine risk in a series of presentations. The three of us mapped out a course of six lectures on the idea of the divine risk and I invited the contributors to this book to join us in the search. They all said 'yes' to the invitation and the lectures took place in Lent 1989 in the Royal College of Physicians in Edinburgh to packed audiences.

Bishop David Jenkins and Canon Rowan Williams were

asked to develop the idea of risk and the doctrine of God, while Archbishop John Habgood and Provost David Edwards were asked to apply the concept of risk to the life of the Church. A. N. Wilson and Elizabeth Templeton were asked to address the topic with reference to the individual or the self. The result was a memorable series of lectures, now edited and adapted into this book, with an introductory chapter from me.

The book might have been longer but for an unforeseen technical hitch. Part of the excitement of the evenings was the discussion that followed each lecture, the whole evening's proceedings being recorded. We learnt after the first night that the lecturer had to repeat the questions from the floor before answering, because our recording equipment wasn't picking them up. Unfortunately, the discussion that followed Bishop David Jenkins' lecture was largely inaudible, except for his trenchant and illuminating replies. We spent days trying to figure out the inaudible questions from Bishop Jenkins' highly audible replies, but it was an exercise that totally defeated us, though the existing tape would provide some theological student with an exciting example of the higher hermeneutic: 'If these are Bishop Jenkins' replies, what do you think the questions were?'

Anyway, we decided that if we couldn't include the discussion that followed all the lectures we ought to omit the discussions entirely. We hope that the book will stimulate thought on a topic that is not only theoretically fascinating, but is profoundly challenging both to Christians and the Church.

RICHARD HOLLOWAY
*Edinburgh, February 1990*

# Introduction

## The Right Revd Richard Holloway

### Bishop of Edinburgh

We occasionally read reports of builders, excavating old foundations, who discover bombs buried since the Second World War. Something similar often happens with certain explosive parts of Scripture, though there is a difference. In the case of the bomb on the building site, it has lain there hidden and unknown; but in the case of Scripture the explosive part is so well known that the invisibility of familiarity has cloaked it and only the shock of determined exposition really brings it before our eyes. Throughout Christian history certain sayings and images from Scripture have operated like this again and again. The narratives are repeated endlessly through time, but every now and again one person hears them with an explosive freshness and something great results: Anthony of Egypt hears Christ's exhortation to sell all and follow him, and the great tradition of Christian monasticism is born; Martin Luther, wrestling with the great letter to the Romans, hears for the first time the revolutionary doctrine of justification by faith, and the unity of medieval Christendom is shattered. Scripture is very like a large building site littered with traps and concealed explosives. Three of the most powerful and reverberant passages of Scripture are:

*Mark 10:35–45*

James and John, the sons of Zebedee, approached him and said, 'Teacher, we should like you to do us a favour.' 'What is it you want me to do for you?' he asked. They answered, 'Allow us to sit with you in your glory, one at your right hand and the other at your left.' Jesus said to them, 'You do not understand what you are asking. Can you drink the cup that I drink, or be baptized with the baptism I am baptized with?' 'We can,' they answered. Jesus said, 'The cup that I drink you shall drink, and the baptism I am baptized with shall be your baptism; but to sit on my right or on my left is not for me to grant; that honour is for those to whom it has already been assigned.'

When the other ten heard this, they were indignant with James and John. Jesus called them to him and said, 'You know that among the Gentiles the recognized rulers lord it over their subjects, and the great make their authority felt. It shall not be so with you; among you, whoever wants to be great must be your servant, and whoever wants to be first must be the slave of all. For the Son of Man did not come to be served but to serve, and to give his life as a ransom for many.'

*Matthew 5:1–11*

When he saw the crowds he went up a mountain. There he sat down, and when his disciples had gathered round him he began to address them. And this is the teaching he gave:
'Blessed are the poor in spirit;
the kingdom of Heaven is theirs.
Blessed are the sorrowful; they shall find consolation.
Blessed are the gentle;
they shall have the earth for their possession.
Blessed are those who hunger and thirst to see right prevail;
they shall be satisfied.
Blessed are those who show mercy;
mercy shall be shown to them.
Blessed are those whose hearts are pure;
they shall see God.
Blessed are the peacemakers;
they shall be called God's children.
Blessed are those who are persecuted in the cause of right;
the kingdom of Heaven is theirs.
Blessed are you when you suffer insults and persecutions and calumnies of every kind for my sake.'

# INTRODUCTION

*Philippians 2:5–8*

Take to heart among yourselves what you find in Christ Jesus: 'He was in the form of God; yet he laid no claim to equality with God, but made himself nothing, assuming the form of a slave. Bearing the human likeness, sharing the human lot, he humbled himself, and was obedient, even to the point of death, death on a cross!'

What are these extraordinary texts telling us about the nature of God and the encounter of the divine mystery with human history? I would like to suggest an approach. The human appetite for power and control seems, paradoxically, to be an expression of human insecurity. Many of the most ambitious people in history have been driven by an insatiable sense of insecurity and inferiority that even the achievement of power and success is incapable of placating. But we don't have to study the pathology of human history to encounter the phenomenon; we can find it in ourselves. Certainly, as I look back on my own history as a parent, as a minister in the Church, as a leader, I can see many ways in which my insecurities made me try to control others and to exercise power over them in an insecure way. Most people, if they are honest, will detect themselves doing this in their role as parents. Children are extensions of ourselves. We feel emotionally and personally invested in our children, so that judgements of them are felt to be judgements of ourselves. Most parents control and limit their children in many ways, often for their own good, it is true, but just as often because they are afraid that their behaviour or indiscipline will reflect badly upon themselves. This anxiety to have our children behave well and be perfect models of obedient childhood tells us much about our own fears, insecurities and anxieties in the face of the criticism of others.

I noticed a similar anxiety in myself when I first started training curates. I wanted to be a conscientious and responsible teacher, but in supervising them I projected onto them many of my own failures and inconsistencies. So afraid was I of failure and indiscipline in my early years as a trainer, that I was frequently oppressive and regimental in my supervision. At one time I even tried to fit my curates out in a parish uniform. I acquired three superannuated Glasgow police bikes, with immensely heavy frames and only one gear, a job lot of dark navy blue firemen's trousers and navy blue donkey-jackets, and set my curates thus clad cycling all over Edinburgh and its seven hills. There was a certain redeeming craziness in it that makes it almost bearable in retrospect, but behind it there lay a need to control the lives of others rather than run the risk of their wasting time and refusing to work. Allowing them greater say and greater freedom would have risked the tight efficiency of the operation. Far better, therefore, to control the shots myself. It is, after all, as our Lord told the apostles, the way of the world. But whether we call it line-management, exercising authority, or 'Father knows best', behind it all there often lurks the kind of fear and uncertainty that is threatened by the empowerment of others.

'But it shall not be so among you,' said Christ. Apparently God's nature is not like this. Our rebellions, insecurities and secret anxiety at our own failings force us to grasp the reins tightly, but it is not so with God. Rather than clinging to the divine nature and its authority, Christ empties himself and takes the form of a servant. And the model of divine self-emptying in the incarnation is itself a recapitulation of the great act of creation. What is creation but a great act of letting-be, the primordial instance of the divine nature going forth from itself to empower a world? Creation is the very paradigm of *risk*, the supreme example of the vulnerability of love. The eternal Trinity did not cling to its own eternal pattern of mutuality in love, but went forth from itself into time and space and thus prefigured its own crucifixion. And the mission of Christ in all its mystery seems to have been the setting-up on earth of an image of that eternal self-emptying, an alternative society that contradicted the way of the world in its fears and insecurity, in its control games and power plays.

Scripture is full of metaphors of this trace element of the divine in history: the remnant that remains of the exiled nations; the few faithful among the apostate multitude; the leaven in the loaf, the salt in the dish; traces of the kingdom of heaven on earth reflecting the nature of God, not of the world; based not on control or force, but on their reversal.

This strategy of reversal is seen at its most bewitching in the Beatitudes, those happy reversals of the world's pattern. In the upside-down kingdom of God it is the poor who are happy, the mourners, the gentle, the persecuted and the oppressed. Christ was the exemplification of this radical reversal of the world's way. He reversed all the world's hierarchies in his own nature. As the divine Word he overturned human expectations of the powerful by his great act of divine self-emptying. And this law of kenosis ruled his conduct. The society of his day was rigidly stratified. At the top of the totem pole stood the patriarch, at the bottom was the child. It was the child whom Jesus set in the midst as the exemplar of the kingdom of heaven, to the consternation and irritation of his followers. He did the same thing with women, who were also well down the pecking order. In his revolutionary teaching about divorce he gave women the same rights in marriage as their husbands. Women belonged to their fathers until they were traded to their husbands; they were marriage property and, however cherished they were by their husbands, they had distinctly fewer rights than men. By his doctrine of marriage, by calling women to be his disciples and his open relationship with them, Jesus challenged the hierarchies of his day, reversed the power structure and emptied it of its pretence and insecurity. He did the same with the poor of the land, who were by definition almost outside the covenant of God, because of their impurity and racial inferiority. Yet, he called them blessed and set them up as types of the true contemplative. Jesus put the last first and the first last. In the great Song of Mary we are told that God has 'put down the mighty from their seat and exalted the humble and meek'. In Jesus Christ he has reversed worldly hierarchies and set up in time a colony of eternity.

This revolutionary understanding of power has many consequences and implications for Christians at the personal and corporate level. At the personal level, it draws us to acts of radical self-examination, especially in our use of power. But it would be a mistake to see the divine refusal to cling to power as a type of weakness and to conclude that Christians are called to a kind of passivity. The reality is much more complicated than that. Christians, in fact, are called to be strong; but it is the strength that resides in gentleness and the refusal to control or manipulate others out of fear or lust. Christians know that they are often called to positions of leadership, especially prophetic leadership, in and to the world. The great challenge for Christians is to provide a model of leadership that is not according to the pattern of the world's clinging to power and control; and since much of this has to do with inner insecurities and anxieties, the challenge for Christians is to learn how to de-egotize leadership, to find a model of kenotic leadership which leads for the sake of truth, for the sake of love, and not for any more complicated inner motive to do with the satisfactions of the exercise of power itself. We are called to radical acts of self-knowledge, therefore, so that we can detect how we are using the power that is given to us in unhealthy, controlling, egotistical ways. The relationships in which power and control become ascendant are seen on the personal level between parents and children, between the partners in marriage or stable relationships, or at work; and it is against that background that we must examine our record. And the same is true of relations not only between Christians but between Christian communions, Christian churches, Christian denominations.

It is no accident, I believe, that the emergence of a new level of commitment to the ecumenical pilgrimage coincides with a rediscovery of the theology that stresses the ungrasping, uncontrolling nature of the God who frees us to be ourselves. If we were to allow this radical understanding of God's nature to influence us it would have a revolutionary effect not only on us as individuals, but also upon the churches we come from. We would no longer seek to hold on to power or the control of our institutional identities but would, rather, struggle to lay them aside, to empty ourselves of them, in order that we might take the form of servants and humble ourselves, even unto death, the death of the forms and structures of the old age of power and control, insecurity and self-protection.

At the moment relationships between the churches are modelled on power politics, rather than on the nature of the God who abjures power. There are two basic forms of the ecclesiological power-play. There is the Catholic power-play. Churches that play this card say to others: 'You don't have full

sacramental efficacy, but we do. Our ministers are real ministers, but yours are "pretend" ministers.' Catholics say this to
Anglicans, who say it to Presbyterians, Methodists, Baptists,
and so on. It is what we might call 'macho-sacramentalism'. The
other power-play is the verbal or propositional one: 'Unless you
profess your faith in this vocabulary and conform to this set of
emotional and psychological experiences, you are not a Christian.' This is the kind of thing that Evangelicals say to liberals
or radicals. There are lots of other power games we play, and
they all reflect, not the mind of Christ, but the mind of the
world and of those who rule and lord it over the Gentiles.

Finally, Christ's pattern and example provide each Christian
community with a radical agenda, given the centrality of children to the kingdom of heaven. The Christian community has
to ask itself all sorts of questions about its attitude to the
children in its midst. This is more than providing entertainment
or edification for them; it will call us to a radical reappraisal
of our eucharistic policies and admission to communion. In
this most sacred and mysterious area, the Church guards and
controls the sharing of the crucified body of Christ, which he
gave so freely for the life of the world. By setting a child in
the midst of the disciples, Christ calls us to the *risk* of a radical
policy of eucharistic sharing.

And in his attitude towards women he calls the Church to a
reversal of the hierarchies of the world. One of the paradoxes
in the current debate on the ordination of women is that the
Church continues to reflect the world in its hierarchies of
power. Like the political world, the world in which the Gentiles
lord it over one another, the Church is governed by grey-
headed men, who protect their power bases by shrewd organization and the manipulation of theological argument. As is
always the case where power is centralized, other groups arise
to challenge the concentrations of power and disperse them.
This has happened in the world where the feminist movement
has risen to challenge the dominance of men in society, in
politics, in the workplace. It is this same challenge that is
now placed before the Church. The irony is that masculine
theologians claim that this challenge is of the world and not of
the Holy Spirit, and that for the Church to hear it would be to

conform to the spirit of the age. They do not perceive that the Church merely conforms to the spirit of an earlier age by its rigid clinging to male control. We have inevitably imported the world's philosophy of power into the structures of the Church and it is ironically fitting that it is from the world's own evolutionary dynamic that a challenge to that same worldly pattern should arise. It is from the children of this generation that the so-called children of light should learn. Inasmuch as the Church reflects the fallen patterns of power and control that it has derived from the world, it must also suffer the world's challenge to its own worldliness. Of course, as is usually the case with those who exercise spiritual power, they refuse to acknowledge the real source of their need to control others, and they claim the authority of the God who abjures power for their own clinging to power. This is why those who challenge the way of worldly power that holds sway in the Church must challenge it in the world's way, by argument and organization. But even this is a defeat, an unavoidable defeat that realistically acknowledges the degree to which the Church has become the world, particularly where it protests its spiritual authority most passionately. That is why there has to be a level above this debate that mirrors the world's struggle, because it is on the world's level that the Church finds itself. On this other level no debate will be necessary or even possible, because the Church will reflect, not the world of the Gentiles, but the heart of the Divine Trinity, in which love goes out from itself to empower others and let them be according to the mystery of their kind. The Church lives on both these levels: it lives on the world's level in its organizational dynamic; but it is also penetrated by the disturbing challenge of the Gospel, usually represented in its midst by prophetic individuals and prophetic communities, so that it fittingly reflects the kingdom of heaven where the patterns of the world's way with power are reversed and all worldly barriers are taken away, so that, in Paul's prophetic insight, 'there is neither Jew nor Greek, there is neither slave nor free, there is neither male nor female.' When the Church risks itself in this way it will, at last, reflect the divine life.

# God and Risk (1)*

## The Right Revd David Jenkins

### Bishop of Durham

I suggest that as we begin our exploration of 'Theology and Risk' by way of the subject of 'God and Risk' we must seriously entertain the suggestion that we really have *no contest*. Risk has changed into chance and taken over so that God has as good as vanished. Further, a grave risk now is that *we* shall vanish. This vanishing will be before our time, as we might say, on the biological clock, because we have contrived immensely to accelerate the using up of the limited viable eco-system of the earth and to invent systems of tension, of nuclear energy and of nuclear weapons which can easily render conscious life impossible even before our persistent pollution chokes us off. We are therefore in double jeopardy. What then is there for theology to do other than to evaporate in total collapse and nonsense? Such evaporation will be the brief, inevitable but insignificant evidence that within the time of the earth, itself contained within the space–time continuum of the myriad of galaxies, we are of no statistical significance. Moreover, even at our own limited and insignificant level we have managed to make a mess even of the very brief niche in space–time which has happened to us. 'Theology' and 'risk' and 'God' are all words which have been uttered for the merest moment of a moment and will never be heard or uttered again in a space–time which knows nothing about the impossibility or concept of knowing nothing.

This negation of a nihilism which is obliterated by simply disappearing into a silence which knows nothing of knowing and therefore nothing of the concept of nothing would seem to be the measure and testing-stone of any theological talk

* © David E. Jenkins 1989

about 'God and Risk', if such talk is still to be attempted. The theological task is not to work out a few modifications to a long-established and currently more or less viable scheme so that it may be better adapted for the next stage in its assured existence and task. The theological task is both to face the issue of whether there can any longer be such a thing as the theological task and to carry on particular theological tasks in the awareness that the theological task as a whole is persistently and perpetually questioned and questionable. That is to say that God is scarcely believable in, and that to believe in God is, in itself, a risk, while the God who is believed in is, in himself, a risk.

All this arises because of where we now stand as human beings. With regard to the physical realities of the universe we human beings are scaled-down. With regard to the future of ourselves and of life on earth we are scaled-up. As to the latter – that is, life on earth – we now have the upper hand, at least as far as the possibilities of destruction go. Natural calamities such as volcanoes, or earthquakes, or even AIDS (if that is properly to be described as a 'natural' calamity) can cause great havoc and many personal and individual tragedies. But they do not threaten life itself or the human species as a whole. It is we who do this with our activities, inventions and exploitations through which we pierce the ozone layer, pollute or empty the food-bearing oceans and threaten the very possibilities of rain by destroying forests and creating dust-bowls. These effects may be looked upon as by-products of the fantastic inventiveness, organization and effort by which we have harnessed energy, organized information and communication, and manipulated our environments with their many threats and possibilities, so that we can survive, flourish, explore and enjoy as never before and in totally undreamt-of ways. And there is no telling what more we shall be able to do, if we survive.

We, therefore, now dominate the earth. The survival of ourselves and of the eco-system on which we depend depends on us. We do have the upper hand, even if it turns out to be the sinister hand of destruction. Where does God come in on this?

Yet scaled-up as we are with regard to the future of our sort of life on our planet the earth, we are on a very small scale with regard to the time of that planet, while the planet itself is immensely scaled down in the dimensions of the observable universe. The sort of considerations, observations and systematic speculations which lead me to talk as I am now doing of 'being scaled-down' can be sufficiently pointed to by culling a few sentences from one of the latest and most enthusiastically received of the attempts by leading physicists to explain as simply as possible what is currently the most generally received theory of the universe. This is *A Brief History of Time*\* by Stephen W. Hawking.

By culling these sentences I am quoting them out of the context of the particular exposition and argument of Hawking's book and fitting them into my own exposition and argument about the scaling-up and scaling-down of us human beings in relation to the risks of theology and of God. I am aware that in so doing I am leaving to one side whole sets of important, exciting and puzzling philosophical, theological and human questions which are implied by the material and the theorizing and which are being spotted, refined and discussed in a good many quarters (although not, perhaps, with as much theological attention and participation as their status and implications warrant). Included in my awareness is some recognition of the difficulties of language within the particular disciplines and theories about the physical universe and, still more, of the difficulties of language which arise when one moves out of the (apparently mathematically rooted) language of the disciplines and theories to make statements about 'the world in general' or 'human life' or, as for example occurs several times in Hawking's book, 'the mind of God'.

These difficulties have effects of which we need to be continually aware if we are to proceed with any responsibility and rigour in this whole area and in taking proper, necessary and disciplined risks in theology. For example, consider the problem of the 'lay'-person – that is, of the person who, like myself, is not trained in, or familiar with, even the fringes of disciplines which contribute to the statements and theories we are

\*Published in 1988 by Bantam Press and already reprinted at least eight times!

considering. We are liable to get a language effect which I would describe as 'loose talk'. A simple example of this can be detected in my references so far to 'the time of the earth', 'the space–time continuum of the myriad of galaxies', and so on. If I wish to advance an argument or exploration by talking about the 'scaling–up' and 'scaling-down' of us human beings, then what sort of 'scales' am I talking about, and how do I use the talk to mean not only what I want to mean but also what I am entitled to mean? If the scales are to do with space and/or time and therefore, from the scientific perspective, necessarily to do with space–time, my talk about 'scales' based at least in part on assumptions about 'time-scales' as extended things like length-scales, fit only loosely with the partially understood scientific talk on which I am relying for the direction and weight of my argument or description at this stage in my overall inquiry.

Similarly, parallel or analogous language-effects are likely to arise when the scientist extends his or her talk derived from, and worked out in relation to, cosmological or biological theories to tackling the widest questions of understanding, meaning and hope. It is clearly proper to ask 'if the observable processes of the universe seem more and more convincingly to be patient of this type of description, exploration and calculation, then what are the implications for human destiny, the credibility of a place for God in or in relation to such a universe; and what sort of God, if the notion or faith were entertainable at all, would have what sort of place in such a universe?'

It is clearly proper to ask such questions – and, in any case, no one can stop them arising – but the talk which develops in pursuing them may well become a little loose as it moves away from language which can be traced back to mathematics and computers. However sophisticated and articulated language has been within the terms of the discipline, mathematics and theories concerned, and however amazing and fascinating have been the imaginative leaps and insights by which paths have been found to develop the theories, to move out into language which is attempting to comprehend everything without remainder is almost certainly to be doing something more or something different. Hence the risk – and, perhaps, the inevitability of 'loose talk'.

I suspect that examples of this sort of 'loose talk' are to be found, for example, in the chapter of Hawking's book entitled 'The Arrow of Time'. I am by no means sure, for talk about time is exceedingly difficult and tricky and I have certainly not myself traced out any of the careful analyses and reflections which are required. I register my suspicions, however, as pin-pointing the problem or, possibly, the systematic and endemic difficulty of this 'loose talk' in an area which is bound to be of central importance to any authentic and relevant theological investigation. For questions about Time are clearly connected with the theological and faithful issue of *eschatology*. Is there any sense in which we have to do with, or can have to do with, something which is going somewhere, a process which has or can have a fulfilment? This would certainly be a central prob-lem, if not *the* central problem for the risks of theological investigation and the theology of risk which I am suggesting is required of us. (And, as I believe, offered to us. For I believe in the God revealed by, and pointed to in, the biblical stories and Jesus. I believe, therefore, there is Grace offered to us for facing that which is required.) For this problem translates into the problem: 'Is there a God and does he have and offer a Kingdom?' And this then translates, from the perspective of convinced and exploring Christian believers, into questions like: 'How do we credibly speak of, and live out, the realities and promises of God's Kingdom when human beings stand where they now stand in relation to the prospects and under-standings of life in the world as we now perceive and experience them?' And *this* brings us back to the context for theology and belief in God which I am attempting to point to in outlining how we human beings are scaled-down and scaled-up.

I can now, therefore, continue my exposition of this idea having – I hope – registered and established the case that risk is of the essence of the whole operation. What I am calling somewhat idiosyncratically and possibly confusingly (but, I hope, provocatively and usefully – at least at this stage in our argument and pilgrimage) 'loose talk' is symptomatic of the fact that we cannot easily, dogmatically or with any sort of certainty put together what our minds can tell us about the realities of the observable universe and what our souls long

5

for, or even pick up resonances of, about the possibly humane and godly nature of ultimate reality. This is of particular relevance to any theological task which is, or intends to be, Christian and biblical. For biblical and Christian theology cannot allow a complete dichotomy between what we validly learn about the world and what we hold to be true on the basis of revelation about the world. Revealed assurances about the destiny of human souls and the reality of God cannot be used to deny or ignore this scientific knowledge of the world, for Christian and biblical theology holds, on the basis of revelation, that God is Creator.

Consequently, where we now stand as human beings with regard to established and authenticated understandings of the future of life on earth, and with regard to the location of life on earth within the observable universe, must be of critical importance for our current undertaking of the theological task and our current understanding of God. To deny this is to deny the doctrine of Creation. It cannot be too clearly, simply and emphatically stated that for portions of the Christian Church or groups of Christians to attempt to subdue and ignore the build-up of the findings of Science in the name of the privileged truth of Revelation is not only quite useless but, far more importantly, utterly faithless.

It is useless, as has been amply demonstrated from Galileo to Darwin and beyond. All that such obscurantist tactics do is to force the Christians concerned more and more to the margins of society where they are less and less able to engage the world at large in the name of that Gospel which God has given to us for the sake of all. But it is, still more importantly, faithless and a practical sort of atheism. What the human mind and spirit perceives as going on in the world and in the universe cannot be excluded from the purview of, or the pressures upon, faith and theology. To attempt such an exclusion is to exclude God from part of his world and it is a denial of the biblical and faithful idea of God. We may not know how the revelation of God hitherto, and the present state of our understanding and living in the world can be brought together but it is a simple and basic axiom of faith that the attempt must be made. What will come out of this we do not know and cannot tell in advance of the engagement, but if we believe in God we must be clear both that such an engagement is necessary and that out of it will come a deeper knowledge and a more effective service of God.

To return, therefore, as the introduction to the last part of this introductory inquiry about 'Theology and Risk', to the data which scales us down. Put crudely and simply it is what is reflected and referred to in statements like the following:

> The general theory of relativity describes the force of gravity and the large-scale structure of the universe, that is, the structure on scales from only a few miles to as large as a million million million million (1 with 24 zeros after it) miles, the size of the observable universe. (Hawking, page 11)
>
> We now know that our galaxy is only one of some hundred thousand million that can be seen by using modern telescopes, each galaxy itself containing some hundred thousand million stars . . . We live in a galaxy that is about one hundred thousand light years across and is slowly rotating . . . Our sun is just an ordinary, average-sized, yellow star, near the inner edge of one of the spiral arms. (ibid., page 37)
>
> The present evidence therefore suggests that the universe will probably expand forever but all we can really be sure of is that even if the universe is going to re-collapse, it will not do so for at least another ten thousand million years, since it has already been expanding for at least that long. This should not unduly worry us: by that time, unless we have colonized beyond the Solar System mankind will long since have died out, extinguished along with our sun! (ibid., page 46)

On *this* scale, therefore, we are diminished in a way with which our imaginations cannot cope and yet with which our mathematics apparently can. But the aspect of our reality to which I am trying to point by use of the notion of 'scales' is, of course, even more complex than I have so far indicated. There is the whole matter of quantum mechanics – scarcely something to be taken up by a layperson towards the end of an already long and confusing chapter! It is, therefore, perhaps sufficient at this stage to add the briefest of quotes from Hawking:

> Quantum mechanics, on the other hand, deals with phenomena on extremely small scales, such as a millionth of a millionth of an inch. (ibid., page 11)

We cannot now plunge ourselves into the issues raised by the famous uncertainty principle of Heisenberg, but the mere reference to it only underlines the vastness, complexity and depth with which we all, and faith and theology in particular, have to live as we take seriously 'where we now stand as human beings', as I said early on in this exploration.

Just as we are forced to ask of our 'scaled-up' position as possible destroyers of life on this planet 'where does God come in on this?' so we have to ask of our 'scaled-down' position in the observable universe 'where can God be located in relation to all this?' Our best and urgent way forward, surely, is to reflect with all the intensity of intellectual, spiritual and moral energy that is available to us 'where are *we* to be located in relation to all this?' This question, I believe, if lived with persistently, gazed at intensely and wrestled with responsibly will confront us with an awe-inspiring, strangely terrible and yet dawningly wonderful Mystery which will turn out to be the fringes of the awe-inspiring, strangely terrible and gloriously wonderful Mystery of God.

I am not here hinting that we could 'theologically' or 'faithfully' expect to be able to discover, produce or invent something proof-like about the existence, activity and graciousness of God. Remember, as symptomatic of our condition, the problems of the 'looseness of language' which I have been walking round and not yet sufficiently clarifying in the middle part of this exploration. We have to do with matters which are exceedingly difficult to talk about, except in ways which are loosely fitting, analogously to be alluded to and appropriately responded to by commitment, exploration, discipline of mind and of behaviour, and by wonder and worship.

But *we* do have to do with all these matters. The convergence of all the scales of reality, moral, biological, macrocosmic and microcosmic occurs in *us*. It is we who are aware of the scales.

We have even, in some sense, invented them, although in a sense which reverberates also with the sense that we have discovered them (an issue or sensitivity which is crudely and roughly pointed to by all the arguments and anguishes about objective/subjective).

It may very well be, therefore, that in some basically true and real sense, and therefore in a way which is truly alarming and potentially destructive because it is so real and responsible, we actually are in the image of God – but in the image of the God who is to be wondered at and worshipped in, through and beyond all the scales and dimensions now known to us.

If this is so – or possibly so – and, of course, I believe that it is so, for I am a biblical believer in God who is known in Jesus Christ through the Spirit – then the intimate connection of the theological task and, indeed, of the very Mystery of God, with risk is surely clear. Just as dogmatic science has developed itself out of appropriate existence, so must dogmatic theology. Einstein could, apparently, never bring himself to accept the apparent implications of the scientific theories to which he had made so crucial a contribution. 'God', he said, 'does not play dice.' Similarly, it is clear, theology, faith and worship have a daunting task ahead of them in being brought through the realization that the comparatively small-scale omnipotent God who has everything buttoned up in imperialistic fashion with guaranteed rewards for his chosen is 'not on'. But the Mystery of the Universe, and the Mystery of human beings who know of the Mystery of the Universe, and the Mystery of love and the abuse of the selves who can love, are all very much 'on' and we are in the midst of them – and in some very real way, very exciting way and very pressing and decisive way, at the heart of them.

I must therefore break off this introductory exploration into 'God and Risk' at this unfinished and unsatisfactory stage because I have not yet been able to get any further. I would like to conclude by one more piece of 'loose' language which has, I suspect, possibilities in it for finding a way forward. We have emerged and we do operate as persons. It is as persons that we have discovered all that we have discovered and that we are challenged to preserve the resources of the earth. Is it not also the case that 'time' as significant is a personal matter? (A clue for a realistic eschatology, perhaps, lies here.) 'Risk' is a personal word. (This is, perhaps, a clue for overcoming the notion of 'chance' and getting back, and on, to possibilities and promises of purpose.) If God is (in some – 'loose' – sense) personal, then he will surely turn out to be not only much more mysterious but also, in some sense, much more precarious than believers have wanted to believe. But is this not what love is about? I suspect that Dr Rowan Williams will have a number of clues to offer you in getting further along these – or similar – lines when he discusses Jesus with you in the next chapter.

# God and Risk (2)*

## The Revd Canon Rowan Williams

*Lady Margaret Professor of Divinity, Oxford University*

To say anything of personal weight, personal seriousness to
another person can be like stepping into mid-air: even with a
person you know well. You're giving form, visible or audible
*presence*, to the words that have been jumbling inside you, the
words generated from a past set of experiences. What will they
do if brought out into the open?

> 'Forgive me.'
> 'Whatever for?'
> 'Forgive me.'
> 'I'm sorry, I don't understand.'

*or* 'I love you.'
> 'I can't cope with that.'

*or* 'Why are you angry?'
> 'What makes you think you know what I feel?'
> 'You *sound* angry.'
> '*Now* I am.'

*or* 'So is the problem just your job?'
> 'You haven't listened to a word I've said, have you?'

I offer my perception; the answer shows me how – in every
sense – vulnerable it is. I've committed and exposed myself.
Even a silence in certain contexts is just as much a commitment
or exposure, when it occurs as a response to another.

> She looks at him.
> He thinks: I haven't understood. I can't help. I don't know
> what to say.

* © Rowan D. Williams 1989

She looks at him.
   He thinks: How can I bear my helplessness to be so clearly
   seen?
She looks at him.
   He looks away.

To say something *or* to be silent with another person is to be
out of cover. I've gone public. What (I fantasize) was the
freedom of my uncommitted, uncompromised self is surren-
dered: now it's 'out there', not my property, not at my disposal.
My words make something that others can seize on. Someone
is looking at me now and I don't know and can't control what
they see. Now I can hurt and be hurt. I can show someone a
distorted image of themselves and so show my incapacity for
seeing the truth. I can allow my self to be shown me in a
distorted image (and not know whether or how it is distorted).
   Talking to each other at a certain level is like this. It's
avoidable only by not going to that level, and we're free not
to. But the price of not going there is twofold. First, it encour-
ages us in a lie, the lie that we are free when we're alone,
uncommitted, not dependent: an archangel dancing in a great
void. Freedom is indefinite and solitary: the words and the acts
that give me over into the hands of others are a sort of self-
negation. This is a lie because it ignores what has made me a
'self' – the words of others, the images and acts that come to
me from outside and make up my 'repertoire' of what a self
can do or say. I've learned how to be a human being by
belonging – before I had any choice in the matter – to the
exchange of words and acts. So the second bit of the price is,
effectively, deciding that I've finished learning: opting out of a
life in time. My self as it now stands, under my contemplation,
is satisfactory and can be kept (fairly) safe, but at the cost of
anything you could call growth.
   Since being human is initially a matter of hearing others
letting themselves be heard, the product of others venturing
into the dangerous waters of constructive speech, then the fear
of commitment, of the risks of speech, is a fear of human-ness:
a fear of the kind of reality that human reality is. Without
commitment to the risks of speech there is no love or nurture.

The still, angelic free self that we imagine to exist in our uncompromised insides will be a stranger to the exchanges of love just as much as to the exchanges of fear and incomprehension. And, if so, it will not know how to love itself, only how to protect itself, which is not the same thing. I have *instincts* about looking after myself; whether or not they develop into what the theologians used to call 'proper self-love' will depend on whether I've ever understood what it is to have nurture given me and whether I have the confidence to give it to others. That is how I know what love is, as opposed to the possession and defence of an object or a person.

Cut yourself off from this, and the supposedly safe person left uncommitted inside my skin or my head knows only the defensive instinct; and in a world which is undeniably full of danger, that instinct will have plenty to keep it occupied. If it's never learned the arts of nurture, it will be trapped in perpetual fear. There lie the roots of violence: in the urge to be the possessor and the definition of my self, which means pushing all doubt and threat outside my self, which means the hatred of what I won't face in my own human reality. Societies do it as much as individuals; a society trying to possess itself in security, what's more, does a good deal to breed individuals who know only defensive instinct. Look around.

The alternative is recognizing that my self is made in hearing and being heard, looking and being seen, and that its making isn't over. Recognizing this also means one specially difficult and unpalatable thing. Each step I take makes for me a definite and unalterable story. Not even God changes the past. What I shall be is taking irreversible shape; I have to ask of my acts and words, 'How shall I live with the memory of this?' The first of Eliot's *Quartets* is about this: the longing to escape from the prison of the present moment and its recollections of pain and shame, into the world that was there before decisions, rejections, humiliations – not a true paradise, but the paradise of a troubled memory: the world before sexual commitment, adult responsibility, the knowledge of death. We must leave this garden before the illusion is finally broken.

Go, go, go, said the bird: humankind

13

> Cannot bear very much reality.
> Time past and time future
> What might have been and what has been
> Point to one end, which is always present.

To act, to speak, is to leave the deceiving garden, created by a fancy that cannot confront how I am bound by my past. 'Words move, music moves/Only in time; but that which is only living/Can only die.' What movement there is that is not *only* in time and so not *only* 'living' is the question addressed with uneven success but unflinching candour in the whole of the *Quartets*.

To act and to speak: to know I have a past, made of exchanges and risks, to know I now *make* a past for a future self and other selves. This is the nature of belonging to the world: how we are real to each other. The paradox is that we become ourselves (what we sentimentally refer to sometimes as our 'true' selves) not by burrowing into the depths of inviolable interior reality, but in these acts by which we give ourselves away into the hands of those who hear us, those who may not understand, who may ignore or repudiate.

I suppose that the point of talking about 'God and Risk' is to raise the question of how, if at all, God is real for us, how God belongs to the world we belong to. To believe oneself 'involved' with God, to believe that there is some sense in which one hears and is heard by God, is to bring God into the world of transactions and vulnerabilities I have been talking about. Yet God, as maker of the world, as the context which gives the world what meaning it has, can't be thought of as a member of any list of things or persons. Hence the characteristic problem of religion: a trivialized God or an absentee God? If we settle for the God who hears and is heard, are we settling for a friendly ghost? If we turn away from the God who hears and is heard, we are saying that God cannot enter into the construction of ourselves in an active way.

The Christian religion, like its closest associates, Judaism and Islam, says, in effect: a god who does not become involved actively in the construction of human selves is not of any interest. The God worth speaking of is the God who speaks. To talk of God is indeed to tell a story of risk; but that risk is the only possible way of seeing what it means to talk of a God utterly free and unimaginably different.

The story runs something like this:

A God who is God, that is, free from accident, limit and change, cannot be bound or limited in purpose; cannot be conditioned in response to the world by anything other than the divine life or nature itself.

If there is reason (Jews, Muslims and Christians believe there is) to speak of that life as an unrestricted giving-away of self, we can call it love.

If this is God's nature, this is the *nature* of God's *action*. God's action can only be directed at the equal flourishing of what has been made. *Human* flourishing – it seems – has to do with the formation of human selves in gift and relation (hearing and being heard): so that God's action in respect of human beings is directed towards a specific kind of shared human life and speech.

But it is only shared human life and speech that *creates* human life and speech in new modes; only the risks of belonging that widen the boundaries of belonging. For God to act as God *is*, then, for God to act humanly: in the life of a people (Israel), the life of an individual (Jesus). In other words, if *this* is the nature of God and if *this* is the nature of our world, the speech of God can only become the transforming 'eros' of all human language by being also limited and historical. There is no universal language, only the hope of creating a universal conversation.

God cannot but 'risk' if we are to hear God. God without human language is not the God who actively constructs meaning and hope. But the God who speaks our language is unimaginably vulnerable; in the sense that for God to give what is God into the hands of the world is to open up what is worse than misunderstanding or rejection. It is to risk *idolatry* – the assimilation of God to some portion of the perceived world, and thus an *absence* of God, which is a force of destructiveness and disintegration.

We may think of covenant and incarnation as good news, the reconciliation of heaven and earth. But if God speaks in the world we inhabit, where speech is an exposure, a relinquishing of power (imagined power, but no less real for that), then covenant and incarnation mean the possibility of idolatry: God put to our use, God as a tool for our power. We think, foolishly, of speech as self-expression; but in the real world of language, speech is not the magical showing-forth of an inner essence, but the giving-up of the claim to define a self in isolation. If God speaks, God abandons control on how the divine is represented; because only in this loss is God real for the world. To say that the nature of God is kenosis, emptying, is not so much a metaphysical observation as an understanding of what it is to claim that God speaks, reveals, acts 'for' or 'in' us. It is to see what Barth meant by speaking of a God who can *only* be known as God for us, God with us, *and* to go beyond Barth in recognizing that as a fundamental act of giving-up, not of self-affirmation or self-evidencing – or at least, the latter only in and as the former.

Ida Görres, a German Catholic writer of the 1930s, was perhaps the first to suggest that the risk and loss of the incarnation begins in God's action as God of Israel. Reading the Book of Judges, she reflected, as we must learn to reflect, on the implications of covenant: to be the 'God of Israel' at that moment is to be what legitimates genocide and terror; to be a tribal fetish at the most bloody stage of Israel's development. In being the God of these people, bound in holy alliance with them, God becomes what is not God, becomes a tool of human dominance and violence. Revelation is *necessarily* a revelation of powerlessness to the extent that it is a 'word' spoken in and into the history where words spoken are seized and mutilated as often as they are heard and answered.

The Gospels show us a Jesus bound to speak and bitterly aware of the loss of power involved in speaking. Most sharply in Luke's Maundy Thursday narrative (Luke 22:35–38) we see Jesus at the mercy of those who hear:

'Sell your cloak and buy a sword.'
'But we have two swords already!'

'Well, that should suffice then, shouldn't it?'

The condensed irony of the 'instruction' points to the immediate future: Once I told you to go on your mission with nothing but the clothes on your back, and you did it joyfully; that mission is over and has failed. It is not your words that will save the world, but the terrible event hurrying towards us. Take your money again, take the world's ways, sell your clothes to defend yourselves: nothing will help now. The disciples' answer is another kind of revelation: they show that they have already understood that nothing will help, and that they have no imagination of the coming event that will do what their mission could not. They only know they have failed and turn back to the instinctive isolation of private resources and the menace of violence. Jesus' irony is overtaken, it falls flat. This little exchange *enacts* what that irony is about, it shows the failure of words about conversion or transformation. There is literally no more for Jesus to say: 'Enough!', he replies. At the end of the chapter the exchange is echoed more tragically (67–71):

> 'Tell us if you are the Messiah.'
> > 'What I tell you, you won't believe; what I ask you, you won't tell me. What if I say that now this man here sits on God's right hand?'
> 'So you *are* the Son of God!'
> 'So you say.'
> 'We have heard him blaspheme! The case is over.'

Again this acts out what its subject-matter is. Who Jesus is can't be said in this context: Jesus is asking a question of his judges that they can neither hear nor answer, they ask him a question he hears but cannot answer. What the judges hear and judge is what they have said; the whole exchange is about the judges' power to control the situation in which they speak; and so it is also the 'judgement' of *that* power because it shows the judges' impotence to see the otherness of what confronts and speaks to them. But their control can still effect what they choose: at the level of manifest 'power', Jesus must fail. The power at whose 'right hand' the Son of Man now sits, in

17

consequence of this courtroom impasse, is not that of the human judge. Foreshadowed here is the world of John's Gospel in which the word spoken to or of Jesus is its own judge, manifesting whether or not it simply turns back into itself, into its own hinterland of private power and self-definition; and the word Jesus speaks 'judges' according as it is or is not received.

The discourse of Jesus in the Gospels is itself, then, at risk. At every turn, it exposes itself to capture and definition, its conversational *difference* is again and again eroded or denied, because that difference brings to light the inadequacy of his hearers' capacity to hear and thus to speak. The 'danger' in which his words stand becomes more and more plainly the danger in which he stands. When he is captured, he is silent.

To read now the texts about Jesus is to be more than ever aware of danger and impotence in them. We cannot read about a conflict with the Jerusalem hierarchy without seeing in it the seed of Christian genocide. We cannot read about the power to bind and loose sins given to Peter and the Twelve without seeing the history of the Church's effort to establish a totality of moral control. The cross has been – literally – the banner of 'Christian' armies, and has been an unfailingly potent symbol by which self-hatred is both generated and blessed. Revelation licenses idolatry; the possibility of a new level of truthfulness is also the possibility of unprecedentedly powerful lies. The records of Christian holiness and the classics of Christian literature seem to live on a knife-edge between the two possibilities.

How should you read Ignatius of Antioch's letters, or St Bernard's? Men of costly and exceptional sanctity, for whom the appeal to their own suffering in the name of Christ worked to consolidate their controlling authority, their *unanswerable* privilege? Is Christ powerless in their hands, or does the very appeal to Christlike suffering from the mouth of one who is after all a real victim (Ignatius *was* butchered in the arena) do something to the manipulative agenda of what is on the page? About such a question you can change your mind between the beginning and the end of a sentence. To go on reading such things is to go on learning something of the weakness and the judgement of 'revealed' symbols.

If God is for us the face and words of a human being (how-

ever inaccessible the details of that human life), there is no
wholly innocent Christianity. We are, from the first, caught in
the question of how we shall cope with the danger of the words
and images given us, knowing that they are *and* that they
cannot be God's. This is what we have of God – bits of our
own world, loosely threaded together to make a pattern so
incomplete and tantalizing that we have constantly needed to
make something of it. The Gospels are teasing and endlessly
resourceful documents precisely because they are so transpar-
ently 'making something' of the tradition and yet are at the
same time providing the material for resisting that process or
for starting again. They warn us against their own devices by
showing a Jesus sparing of 'clear' speech, forcing a differen-
tiated and querying response by his use of parable, falling
victim to the non-hearing and mishearing of what he says. The
very plurality of the Gospels tells us about the risk and the
openness of revelation, and prohibits us from settling too easily
with any one hearing or reading. And perhaps it is this that
enables us to speak about revelation at all. God became a tribal
fetish, but the fetish of a people whose very devotion to it
made them grow beyond their idolatry. Hidden within the God
of Joshua and Judges is some critical energy leading towards
the God of Second Isaiah (or the Gospels, or the Talmud): the
fact of revelation may be bound more to the recognition of this
critical energy than to any one crystallizing or imagining of the
God who reveals. In other words, it is the capacity of a
'revealed' image, a historically generated model of God and
God's action, to produce the means for its own dissolution and
remaking that prompts us to think of a true act of *God* underlying the whole process.

   God takes the risk of speech; and that speech is turned into
the ideology and idolatry of the hearers. But matters do not
end there. However distorted the hearing of God's word, there
remains something of what's been said that refuses to be
absorbed into the hearer's world and continues to speak *to* it.
The last word, as we should say, doesn't lie with the hearer,
however often the hearing is twisted into new forms of untruthfulness. Jesus is defined out of the conversation by his judges;
yet beyond his silence and his death, he continues to address

19

the same question. To say he is 'risen' is at least to say that he still speaks, is still free of what is said to him or about him.

There is no avoiding of risk if God is to speak; and there is no simple overcoming of risk. But where it is God we speak of, there is equally no risk of a final dissolution of God, a final sealing-up of the divine in the systems of human power. The history of God's actions with us is precisely a mixture of the precarious and the assured: what we say in response to God is fraught with risk, because we should know what gross and imprisoning caricatures we are capable of: if we have courage to speak, it is because we trust that our untruthfulness cannot finally silence God. To know that as we talk about God is to do our theology, as we ought, in penitence; it is also to *show* what we mean by the loving desire of God to be involved in our story.

The kind of human relationship that survives the risk and the reality of misunderstanding, uncomprehending silence, is one in which we have reason to believe that we have *time* together: our words have not closed and finished what we may be to each other. The importance of the record of the Bible and of Christian history is that it displays the time God has with us, the time in which idolatries are slowly but constantly eroded. The story of any Christian life should say the same thing. Our hope cannot lie in the possibility of avoiding risk, but in the assurance that God has time to work against our self-serving, self-defining responses to God's 'word', God's entry into our human conversation. And this should help us make the transition from thinking about the 'risk' of God's communication to reflecting on our own decision-making.

I've said that the pressure to withdraw from the commitment and compromise of speech cuts us off from the possibilities of love, and is itself fraught with the risk of sterility and violence. The Christian story of the commitment and compromise of God takes this significantly further, in at least three distinct ways. First, it states as finally as can be stated the inevitability of risk if life is to be shared. If the world's maker, the freedom that generates life itself, refuses to avoid risk by the imposition of divine control upon the divine dealings with us, we have no excuse for supposing that risky word and action can be avoided without also avoiding reality as made by God. Second, it sets our risky and painful transactions within the context of an abiding hope: we all have an interlocutor whose time and resource do not run out, who returns patiently to confront and probe every distortion we may project. We are *authorized* to commit ourselves by the hope that our commitments, however mistaken, will not block the liberty of God to go on addressing us. Third, we may expect not to encounter God's address in those persons or situations where risk is absent. This is not to dramatize encounter with God, to be caught up in a silly rhetoric of faith as an 'adventure', but simply to observe that whatever suggests to us that self-definition in a vacuum is possible, or that human beings can cultivate their welfare on their own terms is a situation where God is not. Jesus was remembered as saying, 'Blessed are the poor' or 'poor in spirit': whichever version is preferred, both suggest that those attuned to God are those who know what need is. To know that, materially or 'spiritually', is to live with risk.

It is worth reflecting a bit further on these two last points. Christians are very much given to imagining that 'taking sides' is undesirable: they long to be able to speak from what they fondly imagine to be the inclusive perspective of God, and defend themselves by appealing to the universal love of God. Official voices in the Church plead from above the conflict for reconciliation between black and white, rich and poor, union members and employers, and so on. People object to the way some irresponsible radicals talk about an 'option for the poor', because it suggests bias in God. But if what we've been thinking through here is right, God is not simply to be found in a perspective that doesn't belong to anyone in particular. God loves the world by speaking to and acting for the unpromising rabble of slaves and gipsies that will become Israel: in that story, God shows what it is to be God in the world – the one who sets prisoners free and who draws the homeless and dispersed into a community where all the actions of common life can glorify God by their faithfulness to the pressure of a divine order. For this to happen in the world as it happens to be is for God to be seen as judging and opposing slavery, factionalism, disorderliness in the relations between human beings. And for God to bring the work of loving involvement to completion, what the divine life is is shown in making completely God's own the life and death of the wandering sage, healer and critic of the false 'order' of his day, Jesus of Nazareth; which means that God is to be seen sharing Jesus' judgement on the static and self-defined religiosity and politics of the Judaean-Roman establishment, and creating the oppositional community, the anti-Temple, the anti-state, that was to become the Christian Church. In a mixed and bitter world, God cannot be invoked to bless anything and everything that is done under the sun: God is known *here* rather than there, God becomes a term in a conflict. Only so can the universal transformation begin: only through the exodus of the slaves can there be good news for Egyptians.

To identify where slaves and Egyptians are now is, of course, uncertain. To say that the woman, or, more controversially still, the homosexual in the Church or in society is where God's Israel is to be seen is uncertain, profoundly risky. To say that – *or* to deny it – is to risk making a fool of yourself. To say it may speak of a hidden servitude to the spirit of a thoughtless and hedonistic age; to deny it may speak of an equal servitude to a frightened or ignorant past. What shall we do? We shall not be absolved from speaking, whatever our words 'speak of'.

But to have spoken in *faith* is to have known that, if we have been seeking to discover where God's opposition to slavery and disorder lies, we have not *decided* to be deaf to God's speech to us. Our words have not sought to drown out God's, whether or not they will ultimately be seen to witness to God's truth. It's beginning to be possible to thank God for saints and martyrs on both sides of the Reformation divide: they risked making a uniquely costly decision, and it is their risky trust we celebrate, rather than using their deaths as weapons in current disputes. Perhaps one day our Christian successors may give thanks for those who took costly or difficult decisions on opposite sides of our disputes today.

But to say this doesn't leave us with yet another bland endorsement of everyone's point of view. To celebrate saints who disagreed in life is to be able to see in both an honesty of exposure to God; a readiness to die for something other than vested power, settled securities. So today: the language that has to be discovered in common is one of shared exposure to the risky words of God, and that is shown only in a shared willingness to listen to and speak with those who most deeply understand risk, those furthest from the power of exclusive self-definition. To understand another Christian at any depth, I need to see how they make commitments, how they listen and respond; how their decisions move them away from, not further into, safety. Only then can I agree or disagree *theologically*.

So we step into the mid-air of words, decisions, promises, commitments. We grow up, join Greenpeace or Amnesty, get married, write a letter, go to communion, vote for or against the committee's proposal, put out a hand, beget a child, say a prayer. Not like a Jesus yielding to the tempter's invitation to step off the roof because we know we'll come to no harm; we may come to harm, we may *do* harm (the knowledge of both is part of adulthood). But it is in that step that we are human, summoned to speech by a creating word. We are human in that risk, as God is God *for us* in risk, as *God* is human in risk, in the precarious signs that are all we have to bind us together.

# Church and Risk (1)*

## The Most Revd John Habgood

### Archbishop of York

One of the dangers in a collection of essays on the same overall theme is that each writer will feel the need to go back to the beginning and talk about risk in general before getting down to his main topic. Hence my apology for doing just that. But I believe it is necessary, because running risks in the sphere of public issues and Christian leadership raises all sorts of questions about who is running the risks, and how they are perceived, and why they have to be run at all. And these are not in the first instance theological questions, but practical ones. I start therefore with two preliminary non-theological points, first about the perception of risk, and secondly about the multiplicity of risks.

Risk is undoubtedly a fashionable word. Risk assessment is big business. Huge sums are spent in trying to persuade people to change their perceptions of risk. How long would you have to sit on the beach at Sellafield, for example, to run the same risk of cancer as in smoking a packet of cigarettes? An awful long time, say the experts. So why do sensible citizens mount protests against one, and cheerfully ignore the other? And why is it so hard to persuade some people to take the risk of AIDS seriously?

The point is an obvious one, but we need to be aware of the profound difference between risks as measured by statisticians, and risks as perceived by the people to whom they apply. The difference depends in part on context and presentation. A society encouraged to believe that eggs are good for you can over-react to the unexpected news that they are sinister packages of salmonella and cholesterol. But then complacency

* © John S. Habgood 1989

reasserts itself as we recall the number of other substances, from salt to orangeade, which have found themselves on the public-health black list. Perceptions of risk need not be stable or permanent.

More important in shaping perceptions is the degree to which those subjected to risks feel they are in control. We accept risks in driving cars which would be totally unacceptable in public transport. Back-seat drivers frequently have different perceptions of risk from front-seat ones. The enormous care taken to ensure the safety of railways and aircraft, and the public outcry when things go wrong, contrast oddly with the resigned acceptance of far more deaths through road accidents. Why the difference? Surely because those caught up in public transport disasters are perceived to be passive victims with little or no control over their own fate. And fears seem to relate more to this absence of control than to the actual pains of injury or death.

Death itself, in fact, represents the final loss of control, and may be feared for that very reason. But as long as an individual still feels in control of the wheel of the car, or the packet of cigarettes, or the shared needle with all its social connotations, statistics can seem relatively unimportant. Accidents happen to other people. And if all else fails, blame the victim.

The difference between statistical risks and perceived risks clearly has profound importance in the exercise of leadership. A leader may see more of the game by having a wider perspective, or less of it by not being at the point where it is really played. A leader may feel more in control than those being led because he is taking the decisions, or less in control than his followers assume him to be because he is more acutely aware of the dangers. He may be conscious of a wider range of risks, but be less exposed to personal hazard. And so on. Risk is not a simple phenomenon, and the model of leadership adopted will have repercussions on the risks which are run and the way they are perceived.

Most church leaders, I imagine, would see themselves as more like airline pilots than racing drivers. Pastoral care is about getting the passengers home rather than about displaying one's prowess.

But suppose we change the image. What about leadership in war? Isn't it the task of a military leader to make the plans, sound the trumpet clearly, and ride into battle at the head of his troops, sharing their dangers and inspiring them with his courage? It is an appealing picture which has often been transposed into an ecclesiastical equivalent. Indeed, from the number of people who quote St Paul on the subject of 'trumpets giving an uncertain sound' one might think that he had been laying down guidelines for bishops beset by the media rather than – as in fact – issuing a warning about over-enthusiasm for speaking in tongues.

Look at the picture of leadership in battle more closely. Essentially what it is about is control and communication, and this is what trumpets and white horses and splendid uniforms are for. It follows that in an age with more sophisticated means at its disposal generals wear battledress and sit in offices in front of computer screens. The great fear in wartime is loss of control, which is why discipline lies at the heart of military life. An army which has lost discipline turns into an uncontrollable mob, and is on the way to inevitable defeat. The major military snag in the strategy of nuclear deterrence is the danger of uncontrollable escalation.

What does this say, then, about the risk element in military leadership? Of course, war is a risky business. But the whole effort of leadership is to reduce the risks by maintaining control. And while this may not entail reducing the risks to individuals who are at the sharp end of operations, there is certainly no implication that running risks is in itself a good thing.

Here I turn for a moment to my second preliminary nontheological remark about the nature of risks, which is especially obvious in the military context. Risks don't usually come singly. The choice is not between risk or no risk, but between one risk or another. There are risks in taking action, and risks in not taking action. In other spheres risks can sometimes be avoided. A car driver who has studied accident statistics may decide to go by bus instead. But a leader, whether military, political or ecclesiastical has no such choice. Everything carries risks – including doing nothing. The task of leadership in such circumstances is not to decide between taking risks, or avoiding taking them, but to come to a balanced judgement about which risks to take.

Clearly, then, the military analogy cannot provide much justification for the view that risk-taking as such carries moral kudos. Bravado can win applause, but it is not really any longer a military virtue.

Yet from a Christian perspective there is something seriously lacking in the account I have given so far. Risk-taking *does* seem to relate somehow to the nature and calling of God. I have said that we are most conscious of risks when we are least conscious of being in control, and isn't that precisely our situation before God? Theologically speaking, the life of faith is a willingness to lose control of ourselves and to place ourselves in the hands of God. We die in order to live. In one sense the risk is minimal, because to lose control to the one who knows supremely what our lives are for is to find ultimate safety, or salvation. But that is not the way the risk is perceived, and I suspect that the loss of control to God can only be real if it is perceived as a venture into the unknown, a going down into darkness, a real dying. And as I am sure you have already been reminded in this book, the work of salvation from God's perspective may entail, even for him, a going down into darkness, a loss of control on the cross.

So what does this say about Christian leadership? Can we find a model of responsible leadership, with all the caution which that entails, yet which includes this element where loss of control is a necessary part of the experience?

There is a superficial, but none-the-less important, sense in which loss of control is all too familiar. Bishops and other leaders are frequently asked to say 'what the Church thinks' or 'what the Church is going to do'. If we fall for the temptation to answer, we very quickly discover that a substantial proportion of the Church, perhaps even most of it, does not agree with us. There is no control over other people's opinions. How could there be? True, opinions may change. The majority of church members may fall in behind a strongly given lead. But church leaders always tread a precarious path between seeking to lead and persuade by speaking out boldly, and losing credibility by ceasing to represent what the Church, in its membership, actually believes. Loss of control in this sense is an everyday experience.

There is a corollary to it in the fact that risks and loss of control within the Church as a whole may not be equally shared. As we have seen, there are different perceptions of risk dependent upon one's degree of personal involvement in the action. The risks taken by a church leader who calls for massive disinvestment from South Africa on moral grounds may look very different to the church member who is eventually going to have to foot the bill. Fears about some contentious church policy, say on mortgage tax relief, may be much more keenly felt by those who have had no direct say in it than by those who have been its architects and spokesmen. A church leader cannot lightly commend 'taking risks for God' without asking, Who is actually going to suffer most if the policy is adopted? And how is the risk likely to be perceived by those who share it in different ways? A deliberate abdication of control for theological reasons, as an exercise in 'Christian foolishness', may entail an enforced and unwelcome loss of control for others caught up in the decision.

The search for a model of church leadership which takes these familiar dilemmas seriously, yet recognizes a genuine theological imperative towards risk-taking, is not easy. In fact the instructions given to me for this essay suggest that it might be impossible. It seems to me that the best way to proceed is through examples, both historical and personal.

I turn first to the major crisis in English Church/State relations this century – the rejection by Parliament in two successive years of the 1928 Prayer Book. It was an event which turned the then Bishop of Durham from a vigorous champion of establishment into an implacable opponent of it. To witness the destruction for dubious political reasons of some twenty years of painstaking liturgical revision, lying near the heart of the Church's life, could indeed have been a pretext for disestablishment. Both Church and Parliament were playing for high stakes. But the worst didn't happen. Parliament maintained its position, and the bishops defied its decision by ruling that the book could be used without parliamentary approval.

Thus the book found its own level among those who wanted it, and was ignored by those who didn't.

It was a fairly inglorious end to what had inadvertently become a high-risk venture. It showed up the ambiguities in situations of this kind, which makes leadership a much less clear-cut exercise then those who clamour for it suppose. Part of the trouble was that the Archbishop of Canterbury, Randall Davidson, was not himself wholly convinced about the book. It had already divided church opinion and much of the opposition to it focused on its alleged Romanizing tendencies. There was also a fatal ambiguity in the motives for undertaking the revision of the Prayer Book in the first place. It was seen not just as an improvement in worship, but as an instrument for enforcing discipline in worship. In fact the great, and unrealistic, hope was that the Anglo-Catholics could be brought to heel by giving them some of the changes they wanted. But in the parliamentary debate the divided motives fell apart, and it was basically the disciplinary implications which decided the issue.

I retell this old story as a reminder of the complex cluster of issues and emotions surrounding what might seem at first sight like a straightforward confrontation between Church and State. The subsequent response of the bishops was modestly courageous. They knew they had to make an assertion about Christian integrity and to that extent were willing to defy Parliament. But in not pressing for the book to be legally authorized they implicitly conceded Parliament's refusal to impose it as an instrument of discipline. So it is not surprising that Parliament took no further notice. The risks appeared great. They faded to zero because the Church as a whole was not sufficiently convinced that this was the right way forward, and both bishops and Parliament were sensitive enough to take the point. Responsible leadership does sometimes have to take risks, but the very taking of them may expose starkly the ambivalences which underlie such decisions.

My second example is also a basically ecclesiastical one, but I use it because I myself had to play the major role in making the decision, and I hope it may help to illustrate the anatomy of decision-making. Was it right to proceed with the consecration of David Jenkins as Bishop of Durham in the face of much vocal disquiet and a petition signed by some 14,000 people? I am not going to rehearse the theological arguments underlying the controversy which are by now tediously familiar. My present concern is with the broad policy implications, the kind of criteria on which a decision had to be made, and the risks entailed in the various alternatives.

Obviously at the basis of the decision there had to be a judgement about what David Jenkins had actually said, what his numerous writings showed he believed, and about his willingness to accept the statements of belief which the consecration service required of him. You have read his essay for yourselves in this book, and you will realize that it is not always easy to know precisely what he is saying, but there is not a shadow of doubt about his Christian convictions.

This judgement about belief, in the decision facing me, had to be set within the context of long-term differences and disagreements about the issues he had raised, and the general unwillingness of the Church, particularly the Church of England, to put the opinions he was expressing out of bounds. What was at stake, therefore, was not some general lowering of all doctrinal standards, but a recognition of very ancient areas of dispute.

I then had to consider the possible alternatives to consecrating him. The most seductive of these was the request that the consecration should be delayed to allow the General Synod to debate the issue. The Synod was in fact due to meet a few days after the date fixed for the consecration, so the delay need not have been inordinately long, but I saw three dangers. First, the Synod would be launched into an ill-prepared debate on a subtle theological issue, thus reinforcing the assumption, which I wished to resist, that doctrine is somehow dependent on synodical votes; it was also highly unlikely that the Synod would be able to come to a clear decision. Secondly, to refer the matter to the Synod would have undermined a fundamental principle of episcopacy, namely that the bishop takes final responsibility for those he ordains; it is one thing for General Synod to lay down instructions and guidelines, but it is quite another for a body of that kind to make judgements about an individual. Thirdly, and more generally, the decision not to consecrate, or to postpone consecration, would have been perceived as signalling to the Church at large that the doctrinal tests already entailed in consecration were not sufficient. To imply that only one particular interpretation of a long-disputed issue could be allowed of its bishops would in my view have reduced the comprehensiveness of the Church of England to a degree which would threaten many of its ablest teachers and scholars.

I fully recognized the opposite danger of being perceived as signalling that the Church was open to any kind of doctrinal reinterpretation, however wild, and this is a tune which some have played vigorously ever since. It simply illustrates what I was saying earlier, that most real decisions entail a balance of risks.

All this had to be weighed, in consultation with senior colleagues, but ultimately alone. I also had to look carefully at the real nature of the opposition, and I therefore made no decision until I had received, and had had time to study, the actual petition delivered to me. It revealed very clearly its origins in a fairly small number of parishes which had mustered a high proportion of signatories.

Forgive this long personal explanation. I tell the story because it illustrates the different perceptions of risk in a confused and difficult situation. Some felt the very nature and credibility of the Church of England were at stake, and whichever way the decision went there would have been an outcry from those disappointed. My own perception of it was much more low-key, perhaps the result of knowing the personalities concerned, and being closer to the events themselves, and therefore feeling that the risks were being exaggerated. I think it is fair to claim that my main concern was to weigh arguments rather than risks, though the assessment of risks was included within the arguments. But I was certainly not conscious of deliberately courting risks under some kind of theological imperative. I saw myself, not as inviting theological adventurism, which is the way my decision has often been represented, but as defending a tradition which was under attack. To revert to an earlier comparison, it was the role of airline pilot which was predominant. My job was to complete the journey with the least possible damage.

I turn to a third and more topical example, and one with a more directly political content – the issue of sanctuary. I am not here concerned with the rights or wrongs of particular cases but with the general questions. Is it right for individual Christians or local churches to step outside the law in sheltering illegal immigrants or those seeking asylum who are felt to have been unfairly treated? And what should be the attitude of official church bodies to them if they do? Behind these questions there lie nearly two decades of officially expressed Christian concern about the present immigration laws and the way some of them are administered; and also, it has to be said, a conviction shared with the Government and with virtually all political parties that one of the aims of the law should be to promote good race relations. Opinions differ on whether these are best promoted by a generous immigration policy, or by a strict one. There are also the differing perceptions of those who are personally distant from the problems, and those who mix daily with immigrants who are fearful or resentful about the way the policy applies to them. The difficulties are further compounded by disagreements over the risks of returning some nationals to their own countries.

Given this scenario, at what point, if any, does it become permissible, or perhaps even an obligation of conscience, for Christians who are deeply involved with particular hard cases to break the law? Is this one of those foolish actions which displays the mind of Christ? Or is it merely stupid, and likely to do more harm than good?

My own instinctive reaction, as one more likely to be sitting in committee discussing the matter at a distance than sitting in a house with someone on the run from the police, is to say that the law has to be obeyed. And I would defend that judgement against special pleading from hard cases on the grounds that in the long run far more damage is done to far more people by undermining respect for law – even if it is a bad law – than by denying sanctuary to an individual who has fallen foul of it. This is a utilitarian argument, as most political arguments are. In the end responsible leaders, whether in Church or State, have to weigh up consequences and set individual feelings within the larger context of the common good.

But other Christians may, and do, react quite differently. They will point to Christ's concern for the individual, to his place alongside the weakest and most vulnerable members of society, and to the need for prophetic protest when laws are felt to be unjust. Prophetic protest need not itself entail breaking the law, and there may be general agreement about the Christian obligation in democratic countries to work for the repeal of laws which are believed to be unjust. But sometimes it is not possible to wait. Individual need, it will be claimed, takes precedence over abstract principle. Is it really true that defiance of the law in this or that particular instance threatens the fabric of law as such?

The argument can twist back and forth various ways. One form of it made familiar in industrial disputes is 'The other side pushed me into it. The common good requires that injustice, even if it is embodied in law, should not be tolerated.' But the counter to that argument is the question, Are we as individuals, surveying only part of the scene, in a position to decide what is just or unjust except through the normal democratic processes? If one man's justice is another man's injustice, then democratic political decision-making may perhaps be the only way of achieving a fair balance.

I have watched serious-minded and socially-conscious Christians divide along precisely these lines. I suspect the divisions may have something to do with church tradition, with establishment or dissent, with temperament and personal experience, and with the degree to which individuals feel that they have or have not alternative methods of influencing the situation. A sense of powerlessness can breed extremism; whereas inner knowledge of the workings of government can breed excessive caution.

Perhaps it is healthy that there should be different Christian perceptions of the right thing to do. Our churches would be immeasurably poorer without those willing to put themselves at risk in response to a personal call made upon their consciences. It is a very different and much harder thing for churches as such, or for church leaders, to step deliberately outside the law, because this takes the action out of the realm of individual conscience and into the realm of church policy. And a *policy* of breaking the law is much more socially destructive than an individual infringement. Democracy and the rule of law are such fragile institutions in our modern world that policies which threaten them need exceedingly strong and urgent justification.

My fourth example is familiar and well-worn, but I think it illustrates usefully the pitfalls in different approaches to a major public issue. I tell only that part of the story in which I have been directly involved.

In 1981 I was invited by the World Council of Churches to chair an international hearing on nuclear weapons. It was a fascinating exercise, lasting a week in front of the world's TV cameras – a high-risk venture in itself. We had an international panel of some twenty distinguished people, and we invited experts from all over the world, but especially from the USA and the USSR, to give evidence and be questioned by the panel. The proceedings were eventually published in a fat volume entitled *Before it's too Late*, which was packed with technical evidence and argument. The report of the panel itself, which prefaced it, had a very different tone. My careful draft, written mostly at 3 o'clock in the morning, had been savaged, filled out with radical and uncompromising denunciation of nuclear weapons as such, and contained the strongest possible language about their very possession being a crime against humanity. Why? Not because this extreme view followed naturally from the flow of argument throughout the week, but because at this point radical Christian conscience took over, helped out by rigorous prompting from nationals who were not members of the nuclear club. 'If we say anything less than this', it was asserted, 'we shall not be heard.' It was this statement which was then further radicalized by the 1983 Vancouver Assembly, and has acted ever since as a rallying-point for peace movements all over the world.

Meanwhile, back at the ranch, the Church of England had been working on its own report, *The Church and the Bomb*. It was in many ways an excellent document, carefully argued, rooted in traditional 'just war' theology, a bit over-optimistic perhaps in its interpretation of East–West relationships, and full of sound practical advice about improving relations and reducing dependence on nuclear weapons. But one recommendation stood out, which led to all the remainder being ignored, namely the advice that Britain should move tentatively in the direction of unilateralism.

There was enormous publicity, and signs of government agitation. The whole of the Synod debate on the report was televised live. And the result was a well-publicized defeat for unilateralism. The Bishop of Salisbury, Chairman of the Working Party, commented afterwards on his dilemma. It was the risky recommendation which had aroused the interest and gained the publicity, but had also led to the virtual dismissal of the many other important things the report was saying. His subsequent reflection was that it might be best to concentrate on asking pertinent questions rather than put forward concrete political proposals; but this is easier said than done.

A follow-up to *The Church and the Bomb*, *Peacemaking in a Nuclear Age*, was published in 1988. This is by far the most politically perceptive of the three documents. It is full of interesting theological reflection on such topics as hope, the acknowledgement of one's limitations, and internationalism, and contains a valuable discussion of patriotism. It gave rise in the Synod to a solid but unspectacular debate hardly noticed by the media. If used wisely by the churches it could have great educational potential. It may surreptitiously influence government thinking. But it has caused no stir, and the Church of England has gained little public credit for it.

I am left with the question, Which of these three has done most for the kingdom of God? If our task is to change the world, not just speak to it, which style and method is most effective?

One conclusion I am driven to in all these examples is that churches as such are difficult to capture for a single cause and are probably unwise if they allow themselves to be overpersuaded. Individuals can rightly and properly devote all their energies in one direction. Churches can seldom do this, not just because they contain many individuals who are unlikely to agree, but because they have to be concerned with the totality of the Gospel in a total environment. And that makes for diversity. And it makes church leaders prudent.

So what does all this tell us about risk? It tells *me* that risk is not perhaps the most useful category in which to analyse such complex issues. Unless we want to stand right outside the political process and simply make gestures from afar, the careful weighing of arguments and the risks attached to different policies has to be part of any sensible decision-making. And any assumption that the most Christian policy is the one which entails taking most risks for God presupposes that we know what the mind of God is before we have weighed the arguments.

I believe a more fruitful way to meet the concern which underlies my topic in this chapter is through the concept of moral courage. It has the advantage of a long history as a Christian virtue. It is an attribute of people, rather than some quasi-mathematical entity more at home in the world of cost-benefit analysis than in the world of grace and vision. And it avoids the unspoken assumption that risk-taking is somehow good in itself, as if the Church has need of spiritual adrenaline to assure itself that it is alive. Moral courage is rooted in convictions and intentions, and is called out by circumstances rather than displayed for its own sake. It may be significant that in traditional moral theology it finds its place alongside prudence, temperance and wisdom as part of the natural soil in which faith and hope and love can grow. Winston Churchill, when asked which of the Christian virtues was the greatest, replied: 'Courage – for it is the only one which guarantees the rest.' If St John was right in saying that perfect love casts out fear, then that surely makes courage and love into bedfellows.

I want a courageous Church, a Church which can discern when fundamental principles are at stake, and stick to them; a Church which does not feel the need to advocate foolish policies for the sake of being different; and a Church resilient enough to cope with internal differences, without losing that sense of purpose which gives it its overall identity.

I return to Churchill who in his delightful little book on painting described the terror of facing a white canvas and making the first brush stroke. Don't dab at it, said Churchill, and use plenty of colour. Those first strokes will set the tone of the painting. Much will have to follow in the way of correction, refinement, the elaboration of detail. But the essential factor in starting is boldness.

There is a lesson here for our churches. We mustn't be afraid of the bold stance, the sharp judgement, the over-simplified contrast. But neither must we imagine that it is the whole picture. There is a special kind of courage in starting, and this is why those prophetic characters who draw attention to some great need or some moral outrage deserve special honour. But there is also the kind of courage required to make more subtle brush strokes, to fill in the detail and to finish; to translate prophetic vision into real policies. It is a courage more akin to steadfastness than to bravado, but no less precious in God's sight. The art of leadership entails knowing how to combine them.

# Church and Risk (2)*

## The Very Revd David L. Edwards

### Provost of Southwark

What a strange thing it is that we tend to regard the Christian religion as a fixed object, when in fact it is always changing! It is not like a statue in a museum, or a figure in a waxworks exhibition; look – it moves! Like the human body, it has to change in order to live and perhaps that is implied by calling the Church the Body of Christ. All these changes involve risks, but the biggest danger of all would be timid conservatism which in the end meant ceasing to be active, ceasing to be involved. In religion as in ordinary human experience, there is only one alternative to a life of change and risk: it is death.

The way to cure our habit of thinking of Christianity as something static and therefore safe is to look realistically at its history. It began with a colossal risk. Jesus of Nazareth proclaimed the fatherhood of God and the kingdom of God: that much seems certain despite all the questions which arise from an honest study of the records of his life. By 'the fatherhood of God' Jesus meant that every human life has its source in God's love and is sustained by God's love. Jesus taught a dependence on God that was free of anxiety. Yet his own life, in close contact with disease and other tragedy, lonely and cut short by one of the most terrible deaths that human cruelty could devise, was a long illustration of the power of the arguments that can be brought against faith in a loving Creator. By 'the kingdom of God' Jesus meant that God was taking action to establish his government on earth as in heaven, to bring his battered and blood-stained creation to a perfect consummation. His disciples caught a glimpse of the fulfilment of this promise in the experience which came to them after his death. Yet their

* © David L. Edwards 1989

claim about his resurrection after his ignominious death has always seemed an idle tale to those not attached to the apostles' fellowship. In the eyes of the world the hope of 'the kingdom of God' has been nothing more than an illusion – an illusion which was crucified, dead and buried. The hope which Jesus aroused can be buried as one vast mistake even when critics have not concentrated on the original mistake, made, it seems, by Jesus as well as by the first Christians, of hoping that the end of the present age, which is definitely not 'the kingdom of God', would come soon and catastrophically. It is clear that the founder of Christianity dedicated and sacrificed his own life in a risk. Has anyone ever risked more than this man who died crying 'My God, my God, why have you forsaken me?'?

Jesus of Nazareth was thoroughly a Jew. So far as we know, the Hebrew Scriptures were the only literature with which he was acquainted and Judaism was the only religion he ever considered. He met few Gentiles; in the Fourth Gospel, which is often thought of as a breakthrough out of Judaism, the only Gentiles are Pilate and his soldiers and a few Greeks (12:20). He taught in a Jewish way; parallels to every clause in the Lord's Prayer can be found in the teaching of the rabbis. His knowledge of science and history was that of a Jew of that date and he accepted beliefs such as demon-possession as the cause of disease. What an immense risk he ran by belonging to a particular society and culture, if his Gospel was to be preached to all nations! And how large was the further risk he accepted when (so far as we know) he left behind no writing at all! The Gospels do suggest that he hoped for the imminent arrival of the kingdom of God, but they do not convey the impression that he pinned everything on this hope. What they say is that he expected the fellowship of the disciples to continue after his death, to 'remember' him; yet he never put his teaching into a book, he never drew up a constitution for his Church and his main memorial was to be not in marble but in a meal. He taught by short stories with no moral attached and by epigrammatic sayings which often were exaggerations, technically known as hyperboles. It was a very risky way of teaching and after his death the community which went on walking in his way had to take immense risks if his message was to be transmitted. To pass the message to anyone not in the original circle was itself a risk, as the Church experienced fully when the ablest, most energetic and most effective of the first generation in Christian leadership turned out to be a Pharisee born in Tarsus, who translated the Gospel in terms of his own intense spirituality and in terms which a Gentile audience would understand. But even had there been no Paul and no Gentile mission, there would, it seems, have been varieties in the Christianity of the first half-century – varieties which could not be controlled by the Jersusalem church presided over by the Lord's brother. When the four Gospels were written down they embodied four traditions which were all largely Jewish but substantially different. And the so-called 'pastoral' letters in the New Testament, to Timothy and Titus, record the emergence of what is called 'early Catholicism', the beginning of the institutionalization of Christianity. Charismatic freedom was now modified, to say the least. There was now an ordained ministry firmly in command; a body of authoritative Scriptures; a 'deposit of faith' which contained at least the elements of a creed in which converts could be instructed.

Had Christianity not changed by accepting this discipline, it would probably not have retained its identity amid a welter of Gnostic and other rival creeds. And it would probably not have survived its confrontation with the iron discipline of the Roman empire. But sadly history was to show that the acceptance of this discipline was to lead to systematic attempts to enforce uniformity of belief in a period when the orthodox were themselves to become persecutors. We may agree with the orthodoxy reached by the Fathers and the Councils, and yet also agree that there was at least a risk of moving away from the simplicity and humility of the years in Galilee and Jerusalem.

Part of the risk involved arose out of the use of the Roman genius for organization and legislation. Part of it arose out of the use of the Greek genius for abstract thought and in particular for metaphysical speculation. And these developments turned sour. In Scotland the Reformation was more thorough than in almost all other Christian nations, but I do not need to remind any readers anywhere else of the strength of the protest against the institution which had developed all the arrogance of the medieval Church in the West. Addressing a readership which is not mainly composed of theological experts, I do not need to explain that the theology which was declared orthodox in the councils of Nicaea, Chalcedon and Constantinople nowadays arouses protests not primarily because it is wrong but primarily because it is unintelligible except among people who are versed in the technical terms of the Neoplatonic philosophy of that far-distant age.

Few Christians would nowadays wish to defend, or to revive, the organization of Catholicism in the Middle Ages, and few would wish to insist on all the language in which orthodoxy was expressed long ago. But I submit that discerning Christians should not entirely regret that the risks were accepted. If the Church had *not* welcomed the patronage of the emperor Constantine, presumably history would suggest that it would never have become more than a minority around the Mediterranean and there would have been no civilization in which millions and millions of ordinary lives were at least touched by the Gospel. And if the Church had *not* welcomed the intellectuality of the philosophical theologians, Christianity would have remained at a distance from the world of rational thought – a world in which Christians were to win triumphs. Moreover, when criticizing the elaborate organization of Catholicism or the equally elaborate theology of the councils which defined orthodoxy, it would be wrong to claim that a liberal version of Protestantism is immune from criticism. At the beginning of this century a great church historian, Adolf von Harnack, who thought that Christianity had been corrupted by these Roman and Greek influences, did claim to be able to state 'the essence of Christianity'. But he did so by making Jesus preach a message which was in effect liberal Protestantism, although the essence of liberal Protestantism was the idealism current in educated, middle-class circles in Germany at the turn of the nineteenth and twentieth centuries – an idealism which put all its confidence in God's benevolence, in human brotherhood and in the gradual progress of civilization. Within twenty years of Harnack's famous lectures in Berlin on *The Essence of Christianity*, liberal Protestantism had been discredited by the First World War, when civilization came near to suicide; hatred and barbarity proved stronger than brotherhood, and God, if believed in at all, had to be seen as the Judge and also as the Sufferer. So the conclusion which I draw from the history of Christianity in its early centuries is not a liberal Protestant conclusion. I want to say that medieval Catholicism and Eastern Orthodoxy were risky interpretations of the Gospel, just as liberal Protestantism was to be many centuries later, and I want to add that it was on the whole good that these risks were taken, so that Christianity remained lively in its pilgrimage to the ends of the earth and to the end of time. May it not be that Jesus knew what he was doing when he wrote no book and drew up no constitution to control the development of his Church?

If I may be allowed a personal reference: in recent years I have tried to educate myself by undertaking some intellectual tasks. I wrote a history of *Christian England* in three volumes. Scottish readers will not need to be persuaded that England has not been perfectly Christian, but perhaps they do not fully realize – as I did not, before writing that history – how varied the seriously spirited life of Christianity has been in England since the Gospel reached Roman Britain and was brought back by Roman and Celtic missionaries. None of these varieties was perfect, yet in none of them was the spirit of Christ wholly absent. At the time dissent from the mainstream seemed a nuisance, yet the harvest of the Spirit grew in Christian lives amid the oddities of the Anglo-Saxon Church, the crudities of what was called heresy in the Middle Ages, the persistence and 'second spring' of Roman Catholicism after the Reformation, the nonconformity of Protestants who were divided among themselves and the rise of movements such as the Quakers or the Salvation Army. In each case Christianity was being planted in the soil of some period or some section of English society.

After finishing that attempt to tell the varied story of *Christian England* I asked myself what were the growing points of Christianity in other countries. In preparation for a book called *The Futures of Christianity* I explored with a growing appreciation the planting of Christianity in the Americas, in Africa, amid Asia's faiths and in the islands of the Pacific. These are regions which have become more important than Europe for

Christianity, and in each of them the risk has been taken of separating Christianity from the forms in which it had been expressed in Europe. Of course there have been problems, particularly since Europe has retained a great deal of prestige, whether centred on Rome, or Geneva, Canterbury or Edinburgh. The establishment of Christianity not by the State but by popular support in North America has been suspect; the identification of Christianity with the people's struggle for liberation in Latin America has been suspect; the Africanization of Christianity has been suspect; the acceptance of some Hindu ways of devotion has been suspect; and so forth. But on the whole, the story of Christianity outside Europe in our own century is a story of risks taken and justified. The Christendom of Europe has gone, but before our eyes great Churches of the world's peoples are arising.

Writing that book brought home to me how Europe is now one of Christianity's most difficult battlefields. Many Europeans have come to think that our continent will become Christianity's graveyard. Of course there are other areas of great difficulty, where the churches are in a small minority; I need mention only China and the world of Islam. But Europe is a special challenge. Its influence on churches elsewhere is a part of the legacy of its Christian centuries. It has been secularized more deeply than any other continent, although China seems similar. The dominant European movements in modern times have thoroughly rebelled against Christianity and one sees this whether one thinks of communism or of consumerism, of the scepticism of the intellectuals or of the materialism of the workers; whether one stresses the exclusive reliance on science and technology, or the exclusive cult of the pleasures of the flesh. And Christianity has been painfully divided in response to such challenges: perhaps that is the greatest problem of all. I have recently written two books in this field. One, called *Essentials*, is a dialogue with John Stott, a much respected leader of the mainly conservative response among Evangelicals. I do not say that this response is totally inflexible, but I do say that it runs the risk of getting out of touch with the knowledge and conscience of our own age. Another book, *Tradition and Truth*, is a dialogue with radical theologians who have taken a very different line. These men are boldly willing to abandon many features of historic Christianity when these conflict with the present mind of Europe, and of course they are in danger of throwing out the baby with the bathwater. And yet I also want to affirm my appreciation of the Spirit-filled characters of many of these fellow-Christians in Europe who offer such different responses to the challenges and who sometimes say things which I think are too conservative or too radical. I would not say that Christianity in Europe is dead, for I see European Christians taking risks in order to absorb and communicate what is truly essential in their rich tradition. And I see Christian lives being lived both by conservatives and by radicals. I am excited by the possibility that the Christian community may yet turn out to be the heart of the emerging union of the states of Europe. My *Christians in a New Europe* is on this.

The history of Christianity has formed the main subject of this chapter because it seems vitally important to reassure Christians that they are doing nothing wrong when they take risks. Jesus took risks. The New Testament is a little library full of adventure stories. Even the impressive structures of Catholicism and Orthodoxy originated in risky involvement in Roman law or Greek philosophy. Those who brought the Church to Scotland or England or the rest of Europe took risks, as did those who reinterpreted the Gospel in successive generations. The modern planting of Christianity in all the continents has been one long risk. It would be ridiculous if, after emphasizing these characteristics of the living religion, I were to claim that my own understanding of it is entirely and permanently correct. The books I have mentioned, although they are the best I can do, are poor things. But I cannot close without adding a brief statement, however short and unsatisfactory, about what history seems to show as the heart of Christianity itself, the heart that beats with a life which escapes the disasters. To risk these disasters is good, since the alternative is death. But to fall into these disasters is in the end to fall out of Christianity.

It may seem unnecessary to begin by saying that the Christian believes in God, but even that belief has been at risk in some of Christianity's encounters with other world views. In contact with paganism the Christian may be tempted to agree that he worships a merely tribal god; in contact with Hinduism, that he worships the God whose real character cannot be known; in contact with secularism, that when he worships he is actually giving imaginative and emotional support to his own ideals in moral behaviour or to his sense of awe before nature. But the Christian believes in One God, the ultimate Reality, the source and ground of all that exists or is possible. This Holy One is infinite and eternal and can never be seen or fully understood, but the mystery can be glimpsed both at the peak moments of human experience and in the ordinariness of daily life. Anyone and anything is capable of revealing the presence and power of God if our eyes and ears are open. God is not a person as you and I are people, but he allows and invites us to communicate with him as if he were a person. His continuous activity is often not clear to us, but he *is* active – and not only through the processes of nature. He is the living God.

This One God reveals himself supremely in Jesus Christ. In that human life he reveals himself as actively caring, as loving, as suffering, as always willing to forgive and as ultimately triumphant. God is embodied for our salvation. That too may seem an unnecessary statement among Christians, but in contact with the revelation and activity of God outside Christianity Christians may be tempted to underplay the uniqueness of this revelation and this activity – and in contact with the harshness of life Christians may be tempted to lose hold on the reality that God is love. There is, too, the danger that Christians may be tempted to think that a particular understanding of the incarnation or the atonement is the only one that is legitimate. In order to guard against these dangers, the Christian often ponders the witness of the New Testament to the Jesus who was a man in history. The Christian also greatly values the Hebrew Scriptures, for the Old Testament is the indispensable background to the New, and its prophets and poets prepare the way for the good news of God brought by our Lord and his apostles. What is authoritative for Christians is the message of the Bible taken as a whole, so that the Christian believes what Scripture affirms. Each of us has to interpret the Bible, but Christianity is what the Bible means for us.

When Christians call Jesus 'the Christ' they declare their belief that the man of Nazareth is the Agent or Word or Image of Son of God in a way that is not true of anyone else in all the world's history. We Christians believe this not only because of the impact of the teaching, healing and dying of Jesus as told in the Gospels, but also because Jesus is alive today. After his death something extraordinary happened to convince his disciples of this truth and although the Easter phenomena have remained unique Jesus has continued his impact as the living Lord in the experience of countless people. To those who open their hearts and lives to this impact, he comes as Saviour, guide and friend, and he is found to have the power to transform our lives so that they become more like his. That meeting with Jesus occurs in many places, times and forms, often far outside the institutional life of the Christian Church. But normally for its deepening it requires participation in the worship and life of a definitely Christian community, where the message of the Bible is proclaimed in word and deed, where the normal response to this Gospel is that those who believe and are baptized together celebrate the Eucharist, where the heritage of holy living is received from past generations, where we learn and gain much from our Christian contemporaries, and where we are equipped to love and serve our neighbours and to work in the world so that it may be filled with the justice which God demands and by the peace that he gives. In the Church Christians are given guidance and power by God as Spirit – by God as the creator of new life in the human heart. This new life produces joy, assurance and liberation amid the continuing experience of the world's problems and sorrows. Here is a light which no darkness can overwhelm. Like the earlier parts of this brief restatement of essential Christianity, all this is familiar to all Christians. If it were not familiar, it would not be essential. Yet it is important to reiterate it, because as they learn to appreciate the strengths of other traditions (religious or secular) – as they learn to appreciate the spiritual power of Buddhist meditation, for example, or the moral power of a political campaigner's passion for justice – Christians may be tempted to forget what is special in this tradition. The special thing is that other Christians who have received the Holy Spirit can be to one the continuing representation of Christ, the perpetual Body of the living Christ, the most precious instrument in the inspired construction of the kingdom of God.

If that, or something like that, is essential Christianity, we can see that often Christians have fallen into the dangers – most often, when the uniqueness of the revelation and the spiritual power entrusted to us have led us into pride and even into contempt and cruelty towards those who disagree with what we regard as orthodoxy. But thanks be to God – because of the Saviour, because of the Spirit, it is not necessary to fall into these dangers! For almost two thousand years Christianity has shown that risks may be run when planting the Gospel and the Church in new soil without fatal damage to what is essential. And if the Christian religion lasts for as long as the human race on this planet, the risk-taking spread of the Gospel will produce new worlds of Christian faith and life over the next two thousand million years.

That, I dare to say, is essential Christianity. You will have noticed that I have not been writing about doctrines which are bloodless abstractions or about rules which are an imposed law. I have been writing about human experience leading to a faith, a trust, which is freely undertaken personal commitment, like a modern marriage. I have not said that this process results in knowledge which is like scientific knowledge. Faith always runs the risk of being proved wrong and this is specially the case when our faith originates in the faith of the crucified Jesus. But what is essential is that we should wrestle with a mystery that is greater than us, even if the all-night wrestle leaves us limping when morning breaks, as in the biblical story of Jacob, and even if the agony of the wrestle makes us groan and sweat and weep, as in the biblical story of Gethsemane. To the wrestler is the blessing given and the blessing can be called personal knowledge. The personal knowledge of God! 'My God, my God!' What a prize!

# Individual and Risk (1)*

## A. N. Wilson

### Novelist and Biographer

Most of us, most of the time, want to avoid taking risks, and organized religion is one of the many ways we use to cushion ourselves against life's more demanding possibilities. By regarding our own impulses as dangerous or wicked, religions can suggest to us a way of living which, if followed, will involve no danger beyond the danger of dying of boredom. Religious moral systems – Moslem, Jewish, Christian – have the supreme advantage of removing any element of choice from our lives. The initial commitment is made – most likely, by your parents rather than by yourself. Thereafter, you no longer need to decide what to eat or drink, what or whether to smoke, how often or with whom to go to bed. The Torah, the Koran, Holy Mother Church or the Scriptures will provide you with the key of how to live. Conscience becomes a matter of following a party line. For many religious believers, the reward for suspending moral judgement in this way is that the ultimate risk of all will be removed. Even death will be safe. That unknown journey which some of us regard with such fear has been rendered harmless for those who die in a state of grace. Death, for the virtuous, will be a mere passage to fellowship with God and the company of the saints. It is easy to see what is attractive about all this, but my brief is to write about the theology of risk, and the part played by risk in the path of holiness. Not an easy brief, for as religions actually exist in the Near East and the West, as they are, as opposed to how they should or might be, risk-taking appears to be the very last thing which they entail. Consider the lives of the most pious people you know or have read about. Would it really be true to write on their tombstone that they lived dangerously? Many such people might respond notionally to the idea of the spiritual life as an adventure, with ups and downs and periods of darkness, and moments when we cannot pray. But 'adventures in prayer', as old-fashioned retreat-conductors might once have called them, seem mild stuff when weighed beside the actual risks which people have to take in the course of their lives.

The broker has to decide whether to cut his losses and sell today or wait for the market to come up tomorrow; the platoon commander in Ulster has to decide whether the flashlight down the alley is a child at play or a sniper with a rifle; the woman who is in love with Another Man and knows that if she sees him just once again, she will be imperilling her marriage and the future of her children; the cancer victim must decide with his or her doctor whether to undergo surgery. The lawyer in court must make a snap decision: he knows that his client is innocent, but lacks the final proof; dare he call the prosecution's bluff? These risks, and risks like them, which are being made around us every day make the 'adventures in prayer' sort of risk seem a bit trivial.

Life is an unavoidably risky business anyway. We all know that things which form part of everyday existence like cars, aeroplanes, sex or boiled eggs have a way of suddenly becoming deadly dangerous. It is in response to such a dangerous world, where disaster lurks round every corner, that moral systems and religions have evolved, providing sustenance and consolation.

More risky for most of us than the outer risks of the world is the inner risk of being ourselves. We are the real liability which we drag from place to place and year to year. It is the Others who apparently fit with cheerfulness into the religious systems of the Shi'ite Moslems, or the Roman Church or the Orthodox Jewish faith. We, unfortunately, are too messy, too awkward to fit the mould. And this dichotomy between the thing we know ourselves to be, and the thing which our religion expects us to be sets up some odd tensions. If we stay with religion, it will arouse in us dreadful feelings of guilt, about aspects of ourselves which not only can we not control, but which we could not eliminate without ceasing to be ourselves. If we leave religion behind, we might find that we have abandoned the only system in which we, with our particular background, have been able to think, morally. Life therefore becomes a chaos.

'Do you mean to say to me', a friend of mine answered back through the grille of the confessional in Westminster Cathedral, 'that it is a sin to *be* a homosexual?' He told this story, cigarette in one hand, vodka glass in the other, with gales of laughter. But when the vodka and the depression got too much, he took his own life. The moment he left the confessional and decided to live without religion was a moment which contained far more risk than any quest for personal holiness could ever have entailed.

Religion offers us the companionship of a God 'who alone can order the unruly wills and affections of sinful men'. It peoples heaven with saints, men and women who either never appeared to have had unruly wills or who appeared to be able to keep them under control without much divine assistance.

Saints, I more and more conclude, are idols, and the cult of saints is in constant danger of turning into idolatry, a setting-up in our hearts of not merely falsehoods about what these individuals were like, historically, but also a completely false image of what we and every other human being on this planet are actually like.

Two disconcerting examples of this phenomenon have come my way in the last year of work, one in connection with a book I am writing, and the other involving a film which I have made for television.

The first is the book. C. S. Lewis is regarded with veneration by many Christians, particularly in the USA. I have been an admirer of his writings for much of my life, but it is only in the last few years, working on a book about the man, that I have come to see what a vulnerable and mixed-up figure he was. All that is good and much that is bad in his writing springs from his vulnerability. His sense of human life as an exile, and the spiritual journey as an attempt to find the way home are his hallmarks – they make his children's stories, slapdash in execution as they may have been, possess an everlasting appeal. No doubt this sense of loss, of longing for a far country we can only rarely glimpse on this side of paradise, owes much to

Lewis' wretchedly unhappy childhood and the loss of his mother before puberty. No doubt, Lewis himself when he came to write his autobiography, and above all the story of his famous conversion to Christianity, thought he was telling the truth. He goes out of his way to inform us that the conversion had nothing to do either with the death of his father, or with his emotional life. In fact, the conversion occurred during the year in which he lost his father and was estranged (I would assume sexual relations had ceased) from his lifelong companion and mother-substitute, Mrs Moore. Lewis was actually unable to believe in a Heavenly Father until his own father, with whom he had a disastrous relationship, was out of the way. Belief in God came almost the instant his father died, and provided him with a respectable excuse for putting away a much older woman who wearied him.

It does not diminish Lewis for me to think that his religious development grew out of his life in this way. Nor does it diminish him, for me, to suggest that this conversion, which turned him from a bluff, self-confident atheist into a bluff, self-confident Christian, was only half the story. Having written a series of books in which he appeared to know all the answers to everything – those works of popular theology which made his name – Lewis' life began to be unstuck. He fell in love – wildly unsuitably, as his friends thought, with someone much younger, who was married with two small children. Marrying her meant breaking all the rules, and, as is so very well known, she was suffering from cancer. The marriage was of heartbreakingly short duration, but long enough for them to form all kinds of hopes that the disease had been cured, rather than simply entering a remission.

Which was the Lewis who took the real spiritual risks? The Lewis who knew all the Christian answers and set them out in *Mere Christianity* with unrivalled clarity and readability; or the gentler, hurt Lewis who wrote the *Letters to Malcolm*, the anguished Lewis, crying out to God, not with witty answers but with howls of pain?

The Lewis admirers, I have found, are not always interested in such questions, because they are not always interested in what Lewis was actually like. It would appear that a large proportion of his American admirers are non-smoking, tee-totalling people who have no wish to know about their hero's tastes in these areas. It is probably telling tales out of school to relate what a previous biographer of Lewis told me about his publisher in California. George Sayer knew Lewis for many years and was his pupil. Nevertheless, he was told by his American publisher to cut references to Lewis smoking and drinking. Since Lewis smoked continuously, pipes and cigarettes, and since his colloquies more often than not took place in pubs, Sayer not unnaturally felt that he was being asked to produce an emasculated version of his old friend. Lewis' high-church admirers, on the other hand, who themselves smoke and drink but revere the celibacy of the saints, like to assert, against all the evidence, the doctrine of the perpetual virginity of C. S. Lewis. Even his marriage, according to this doctrine, was unconsummated.

I do not give these examples to mock. They are examples of how hagiography works. And the relevance to the theme of risk will, I hope, become clear before we are done. Let me give you one more example. Again, it came my way in the last twelve months.

A lifelong hero of mine is John Henry Newman. Last summer I made a television film about his life. No dispassionate observer of Newman can fail to be impressed by his faith, his piety, his intellectual honesty and his eloquence. Equally, the same observer could hardly read Newman's letters or study his life without becoming aware of the man's weaknesses, his prickliness, his extraordinary readiness to take offence, his flashes of real paranoid malice, his passionate likes and dislikes. Few men leading a communal life ever took less notice of Thomas à Kempis' injunction to avoid inordinate affections. In those pre-Freudian innocent days Newman, who was cold and indeed totally silent with fellow-priests whom he disliked, poured out love in tears and words to his beloved friend Ambrose St John. When he died, Newman was insistent that he should be buried, not as other cardinals are buried in some cathedral tomb with his hat hanging over him, but in the same suburban grave of the man he had loved so deeply and so innocently.

The attitude of the Birmingham Oratory when it was discovered that I was of this opinion was one of horror. I was implying, apparently, that Newman was some sort of tormented neurotic homosexual. I was implored not to mention the fact that nearly all Newman's fellow-oratorians found life with him so intolerable that they left to found a separate community in London; nor to say anything about the burial arrangements. To do so, it was said, would upset the faithful and might even imperil the cause of Newman's beatification in Rome.

I am sure that nothing I did or said would have the slightest effect on the Process which is at this moment being considered in Rome. But the desire of Newman's successors at Birmingham to have a perfect, equable, uncomplicated Newman seemed to me a bit like the desire of other Christians to have a non-smoking or celibate C. S. Lewis.

It may comfort people to believe in plaster saints, but this is not my idea of Christianity. If we light enough candles to them, the hope must be that we shall grow into plaster saints too, and that to my mind is not the same as having life and having it more abundantly, which is the promise of the Christian Gospel.

Lewis' most valuable Christian insights come, I believe, precisely from the weakness which he knew within himself, and not from his alleged perfection. They came from his missing his mother and his needing the support not only of bluff male friends but also of women. They came from the sense of sin which made *The Screwtape Letters* and the sheer pain of *A Grief Observed*. They came from the moments in his life where he had been shaken into being himself, or where he was prepared to risk himself.

Newman is comparable. The sheer artistry of his Anglican sermons, the mellifluousness of his prose, when he was the cult figure and the highly successful vicar of St Mary's Oxford, provide a thrillingly austere religion to follow. But it is a religion for prigs. It is after he has taken some big risks and been rewarded with rebuttal and failure that Newman becomes an interesting figure. His astonishing decision to join the Church of Rome at a date when, in England, it barely existed, led him into a wilderness where the company and the religion were alike uncongenial. Throughout his Catholic life, Newman felt people looking over his shoulder, suspecting him of heresy, reading (I would suspect rightly) signs in his works of incipient modernism and subjectivism. The sheer intellectual as well as personal loneliness of it broke his heart, but he never wavered in his loyalty to the new obedience. When Charles Kingsley in his blundering way accused Newman, eighteen years after his conversion, of having led a devious pseudo-popish life in the Church of England, something in Newman snapped. In six lachrymose weeks, he poured out of himself the story of his own life, everything which had been going on inside him since he was an intensely imaginative, strange little boy, supposing himself to be an angel and this world a dream. The result was the *Apologia Pro Vita Sua*, a book which follows his progress through the experience of childhood conversion to the rigid Calvinism of his young manhood, the heady dreams, more fantastical than anything he had read in the *Arabian Nights* as a boy, that the Oxford Movement would convert England to primitive Christianity, and finally the steps which led him, Pied-Piper-like, to leave the Church he loved to become the least appreciated of all great Catholic converts.

The book made Newman popular – popular with an audience who had taken no previous interest in him, or who had assumed him to be a spent force: that is to say, with Protestants and freethinkers and seekers. The Catholic authorities were appalled by it. Manning thought that the book represented religion as a purely subjective thing, something going on inside you. He surely missed the point of the book which is that true religion is what we risk doing with our weakness.

In the opening pages of this essay I have described a kind of religion which provides us with a blueprint of how to live. You could call such a religion that of the Law, the Nomos, the Torah. St Paul repudiated that kind of religion precisely because it can only show us our weakness, our incapacity to keep rules. It therefore brings death and condemnation. Paul suggests a much odder and much more radical view of life in which strength is made perfect in weakness. To find out whether or not he was right would involve us in such risks that very few individuals have even set out to try. These individuals are so rare that the rest of us, with our naturally pharisaic tendencies, want to neutralize them as soon as we can, either by dismissing them as lunatics or by making them into plaster saints. Think of what we do with Francis of Assisi, think of the sentimental rubbish which we speak about him, as though kissing the leper was all in a day's work for a do-gooder. Francis was not interested in wiping out leprosy, nor in persuading the world health organization to devote more money and research to a cure for the disease. He kissed the leper because he was in love with God, and because he saw God in that man – especially in that man, especially in the figure of a weak, helpless, disease-ridden outcast. That is the distinctively anarchic and Christian thing about Francis.

The admirers of Newman and Lewis want their heroes to be perfect. They sense God coming through these individuals, speaking to them in their writings. Anyone who then comes along and points the supposed weaknesses of the men themselves must be trying to debunk or satirize two great Christians; whereas I believe the truth to be much odder than that. The strength of Christians is made perfect in weakness. It really is. The distinctively Christian things in Lewis came not when he was displaying feats of rhetoric, but when he was missing his mother, in a muddle about sex, crying for his dead wife. Newman's best book does not come when as a suave and highly successful preacher he has placed himself at the centre of a personality cult. It comes when his heart is broken with nostalgia for his friends, his wrong-headed, but so-much-loved friends.

The true Christian soul is a figure who is prepared to put himself or herself into such a position of vulnerability, the sort of position which most of us get into by accident and wish we could avoid. Saints, if such figures exist, are not people who have managed to get through life without smoking a cigarette or forming unsuitable erotic attachments. Saints are those who love God with such an intensity of love that they do risk everything for it. In the case of each individual saint the risk will be different, but an element of risk is almost certain to have been involved, whether it is the risk of life itself, made by a martyr, or the risk of being gloriously wrong, made by a genuinely humble and intelligent thinker.

To be honest, I do not really understand the concept of holiness, and do not even find it particularly attractive – in the sense of it being a quality after which I yearn myself. I think that I see it in the lonely intellectual quest of Simone Weil, in the imaginative journeys of William Blake, in the heroic martyrdom of Ridley and Latimer. All did as they did because they had God before their eyes, all the time, so real and so vividly present to them, that they were prepared to risk – in Blake's case, a lifetime of neglect and poverty; in Wesley's, fatigue and desolation and rejection; in the martyr's case, death itself. They were all strong, but made themselves weak in order to get closer to their goal, which was the love and knowledge of God.

I do not know God. I am not holy. Why is it that I do not feel excluded from the company of great Christian men and women, although I do feel totally excluded by the language of hagiography and the world of plaster saints? It is for this reason.

Although my imagination cannot grasp it, I believe and hope in the gospel of redemption. God is not a schoolmaster or a policeman, endlessly watching for us to commit offences for which we will be punished. 'For ye have not received the spirit of bondage again to fear; but ye have received the spirit of adoption, whereby we cry, Abba, Father' (Romans 8:15). The Old Testament has running through all its horrors, like a silver thread, the knowledge of this Gospel. 'The merciful goodness of the Lord endureth for ever . . . Like as a father pitieth his own children, even so is the Lord merciful . . . Look how wide also the east is from the west: so far hath he set our sins from us' (Psalm 103:17, 13, 12).

But the imagination cannot grasp this. We prefer a false, angry God, made in our own image of some Freudian father-figure, the God whom William Blake called Nobodaddy. We prefer a God who makes us guilty about our sinfulness, rather than a God who loves us for being us.

Jesus was not unique in proclaiming the Love of God as it is set out in the Scriptures. Many of his words do little more than paraphrase or repeat things which could be read in the Old Testament. But he was recognized, we are told, as speaking with authority, and not as the scribes (Mark 1:22). The religion of scribes, the worship of Nobodaddy, is the natural projection of human beings, the normal thing which fallen men and women will do with their God-implanted religious impulse. The scribe comes into the temple, and thanks God that he is not as other men are, 'extortioners, unjust, adulterers, or even as this publican' (Luke 18:11). The publican has nothing more useful or moral to say than, 'God, be merciful to me a sinner! I tell you, this man went down to his house justified rather than the other' (Luke 18:13, 14).

It really is outrageous. No wonder that even those who have grasped the significance of the gospel of grace most fully have never done so perfectly. St Paul, who in paragraph after paragraph of his letters expounds the unsearchable mystery of grace, the fact that God loves us while we *are* yet sinners, is still capable of tediously pharisaical tirades against any particular human activity of which he happens to disapprove – wantonness, cutting your hair short (if you are a woman), growing it long (if you are a man), etc. And that is because all of us, with our old Adam, naturally want to go on worshipping Nobodaddy. We want to go on saying that God will love us only on condition that we stop being sinners; that the real purpose of religion is to convert sinners into Pharisees. But that is not the Gospel. *Metanoia* or repentance involves a change of mind, a change of intention, a focusing of our love on God. But if it turns the humility of the publican into the humbug of the Pharisee, then it is time to think again. We must have got it wrong.

> If Moral Virtue was Christianity,
> Christ's Pretensions were all vanity . . .

When Jesus went to the house of Simon the Pharisee, no one appears to have been surprised by the fact that the scribe, the moral man of Law, did not extend a very warm welcome to him.

> I am sure this Jesus will not do
> Either for Englishman or Jew.

The Pharisee was too enclosed in his own perfect moral system to wish to welcome Christ into his house. He had absolutely no need of him, any more than the Pharisee in the temple had need of him. It is perfectly possible to live without love, if you can call it living. Into the scene there intrudes the shocking and embarrassing figure of a woman in the city, 'which was a sinner' (Luke 7:37). 'Simon, seest thou this woman? I entered into thine house, thou gavest me no water for my feet: but she hath washed my feet with tears and wiped them with the hairs of her head. Thou gavest me no kiss: but this woman since I came in hath not ceased to kiss my feet. My head thou didst not anoint: but this woman hath anointed my feet with ointment. Wherefore I say unto thee, Her sins which are many, are forgiven; for she loved much: but to whom little is forgiven, the same loveth little' (Luke 7:44–47).

Love is the great risk. Love is what redeems the woman. Love is the thing of which the poor, pinched, virtuous Simon the Pharisee is no longer quite capable.

John tells us that it is impossible to love God unless we also love our fellow human beings. 'He that loveth not, knoweth not God: for God is love' (1 John 4:8). 'No man hath seen God at any time. If we love one another, God dwelleth in us, and his love is perfected in us' (1 John 4:12). Each of us has within our own hidden self a Pharisee and a sinner. The sinner wishes to turn to God for forgiveness and love; the Pharisee wishes to say that we cannot so turn until we have made *ourselves* good and clean and virtuous, by our own efforts. St John knows better: 'For if our heart condemns us, God is greater than our heart' (1 John 3:20).

The Pharisee, of course, is not really a virtuous voice. The Pharisee is a diabolical voice, disguising itself as the promptings of conscience. By urging us to live by rules, rather than by love, the Pharisee creates a moral universe in which God is actually redundant, and love has no necessary part. Christians believe that this voice is not just limiting and destructive, but actually untrue. *God is greater than our heart*. If, as the greatest Christian poet has asserted, it is Love Itself, Love Himself, which moves the sun and other stars, then the Pharisees are not merely prigs, they are fools. They are closing their eyes to the nature of things. Christians are called to believe that love is the principle by which all things cohere, by which God and his creation know one another, by which human beings discover their true identity under the eye of eternity. That is why Jesus is able to make his completely astonishing statement in the house of Simon the Pharisee.

It does not need me to explain why it would be much safer to live without love. Love, however we discover it, and in whatever of its forms, involves self-exposure and self-giving. Falling in love is the most dramatic thing which ever happens to most of us, because we are no longer able to be safely shut up within ourselves. Images of the beloved haunt our dreams and our waking thoughts. Against our will, and often against our better judgement, we think of them, and the experience of growing in such a love is the experience of giving away self to the beloved, only to find it again, immeasurably enriched.

For Dante, this experience, that of falling in love with a woman, became the vehicle through which he explored the entire meaning of the gospel of redemption. It is the supreme example in most human lives of the preparedness to sell everything and buy the pearl of great price, whatever the cost or the sacrifice. But such an element of self-giving and sacrifice is present in all forms of loving. Love, which has the greatest power to console us and nourish us, is also the thing which makes the greatest demands upon us, so that even in friendship, perhaps the most painless of the loves, there is an element of this sacrificial thing, of giving, not in order to gain, but because giving is required of us; giving of time, of help, of an ear to a boring story or a lunchtime when we might prefer to be doing something else. Without such little sacrifices, friendships wither.

The love which a parent gives to a child is perhaps the closest thing to sacrificial love which most of us experience in ordinary life. That is not to say that many parents can rise to heights of self-denying affection for their children all the time. But by taking the risk of having a child, we bring into the world a being who did not ask to be born, and who throughout their lives, until the day they die, will respond to the way we did or did not treat them. Assuming that some kind of bonding takes place at the time of birth or soon after, the parent feels linked to their love in an uncontrollable way. To nourish and protect the young feels like instinct, and one only has to see the parents of very young children to be astonished by the sheer exhausting self-giving which this entails. Would they have taken the risk, before they had children, if they had known how wearing, how simply tiring, it could be? In almost all cases, the answer would be an unswerving, unhesitating 'Yes', for the joy of loving a child is an incomparable, and for most parents, an immovable thing. But what a risk. For very few children believe their parents to be faultless, and most can point to the most absurd mistakes which parents have made, usually in the precise areas where they were trying hardest to be right. It is there, perhaps, that the greatest heartbreak occurs. The parent–child relationship is nearly always flawed, and the flaw will have an everlasting effect. 'Can a woman forget her sucking child, that she should not have compassion on the son of her womb? Yea, they may forget, yet will I not forget thee' (Isaiah 49:15). So speaks the God of Second Isaiah.

In those remarkable prophecies, believed to have been preached in Babylon in the sixth century BC at the lowest point in the fortunes of Israel, we encounter the figure of the Suffering Servant, the man of sorrows (Isaiah 53:3) who appears after exultant passages of great joy, proclaiming the redemption of Jerusalem. 'He is despised and rejected of men; a man of sorrows, and acquainted with grief: and we hid as it were our faces from him; he was despised and we esteemed him not' (Isaiah 53:3) . . . 'He was oppressed, and he was afflicted, yet he opened not his mouth: he is brought as a lamb to the slaughter, and as a sheep before her shearers is dumb, so he openeth not his mouth' . . . 'And he made his grave with the wicked' (Isaiah 53:7, 9). Second Isaiah sees this essentially vulnerable figure, who has removed from himself, or had removed from him, all strength and protection, as a figure who redeems. In his absolute weakness, the prophet sees strength. The ultimate risk of all has been taken, and 'therefore will I divide him a portion with the great, and he shall divide the spoil with the strong; because he hath poured out his soul unto death' (Isaiah 53:12).

When a Christian reads these passages, it is sometimes hard for him or her to remember that they describe a messianic figure in the imagination of a poet-prophet who lived five hundred and fifty years before Jesus was born. From early times, certainly from the time of St Matthew's Gospel (Matthew 12:17ff.) Christians have identified the figure of the Suffering Servant with Jesus himself. Reading about the suffering servant was *one* of the ways in which they tried to make sense of the incomprehensible and awful events of the first Good Friday.

However *we* try to meditate upon the passion of Christ, it is likely that the images supplied by the Second Isaiah will return to our minds; and in so far as Jesus was the last of the great Hebrew prophets, embodying in himself and his actions the things he wishes his hearers to know about God, then this must be helpful. It is not inconceivable that Jesus saw himself, in some sense, as identifiable with the Second Isaiah's Servant.

If so, how does the death of Jesus on Calvary relate to the theology of grace? I am not asking, how can we explain what happened on the cross, because we can't – only mythologies and pictures and analogies come anywhere near to presenting its meaning. I am asking the simpler question, What is the relation between the teaching of Jesus and the death of Jesus?

If the gospel of grace is the essence of what Jesus taught, then the relation would be something along these lines. Jesus taught that God loves us for being what we are, and not for putting on our Sunday best. It is in response to love that we come alive, that we have life, and have it more abundantly; and that is why chaotic sinful people who have not lost sight of love, find it easier to turn to God than those who are imprisoned in their own arcane and rigid religious formularies. So it is only as a child that we find Jesus sitting with the doctors of the Law. In grown-up life, he is a wine-bibber, a gluttonous man, a figure who sits at meat with sinners. Was he coming to preach some esoteric mystery-religion, of the kind which might have appealed to Dostoevsky, which suggested that it did not matter how we behaved, or that it would actually have been a token of belief in God's forgiveness to behave wilfully badly? No. We are not to sin the more that grace may the more abound (Romans 6:1). But nor are we to imagine that morals are a substitute for love, or that we can redeem ourselves by right conduct. Love is the fulfilling of the law. And if we would only risk living by love and not by rule, we should discover the true law of God, which is not the *Thou shalt not* of Sinai, but the spontaneous gratitude which can make a woman pour out ointment over Christ's feet, a lame man leap for joy.

But however often we heard this gospel, we should want to distort it; or, even if we did not want to distort it, we should subtly transform it into its precise opposite. We should want to believe that all those publicans, prostitutes and moral inadequates, having turned over their new leaf and made a bow in the direction of justification by faith would actually turn into humble servants of Caiaphas. Now the world in which Caiaphas has control is an admirable place. It is full of comfortable, middle-class homes, and everyone there is polite and clean and well-behaved, and vice is something which we have left far behind in our own past, or which we read about with dismay in the newspapers. Caiaphas is not exactly a humbug. In his less amiable moods, he thanks God that he is not as other men are. In his more altruistic frames of mind, he busies himself with schemes to make the poor benighted human race more like himself. He will not cease until he has cleaned us all up.

But now he finds in his path a threat to his entire existence. He finds Jesus, who knows that most of us are hopeless cases. We are never going to be much better than we are. It is only in that recognition of what we are, in that realization of the gulf between our inadequacies and God's perfection, that we glimpse the reality of things. Caiaphas is not against us having a few raffish friends. But he wishes that X didn't swear and that Y wasn't such a gossip and that Z didn't get lecherous and sentimental when he'd had a few drinks. Jesus knows that human beings are a mixture of good and bad, and that to remove the so-called bad bits, or to pretend that they aren't there is to remove the essence of what makes most of us lovable. He says, *Sin no more* (or the gospel writers tell us that he says so). But he tells us stories like that of the Prodigal Son, in which the father is waiting patiently for the son's return, largely unconcerned by the indiscretions which enabled him to get through his inheritance so fast. And this is what Caiaphas cannot stomach. It is the way that Jesus challenges the human race to risk stepping outside the safe confines of ethical systems and to venture out into living a way of love.

Jesus and Caiaphas therefore find themselves on a collision course, but because they look at the world in precisely opposite ways, they are in fact planning the same thing. Jesus wishes to show his disciples the meaning of God's love for men and women. He has told them the story of the Prodigal; he has pointed to the example of the woman who poured ointment over his feet; he has told the story of the Pharisee and the publican. But although they have nodded their agreement, no one except the consciously penitent sinners themselves have quite been able to see what he was saying. So, like the Suffering Servant of Isaiah, Jesus must take himself beyond the moral pale, and die the death of a sinner, even though he has committed no offence.

Jesus knew that God loves us while we are sinners, not on condition that we stop being sinners. He knew that in a fallen world, our good and bad natures are all mixed up. So he chooses to die a disgraceful death. It is not a hero's death: he was not making some kind of clever legal point at his trial, such as Thomas More, for instance, was making at his. Nor was he fighting for the liberation of his people against the Romans. For St Paul, who could easily have been in Jerusalem at the time of the crucifixion, there is one simple fact about it which outshines every other fact. It is not what Jesus said at his trial, if he said anything at all, or how brave he was: it is the shockingly simple fact that a man who dies in this way is held accursed by the Jewish law. 'Christ hath redeemed us from the curse of the law, being made a curse for us; for it is written, Cursed is every one that hangeth on a tree' (Galatians 3:13). The only way he could show that he really meant what he said in pointing the contrast between the sinner and the Pharisee was to die the death of the sinner.

> And Caiaphas was in his own Mind
> A benefactor to Mankind:
> Both read the Bible day and night,
> But thou read'st black where I read white.

Caiaphas, who is such a devout man, can see no difference

between a redeemed human race and an improved human race. He will either, if he is an idealist, go on trying to improve us all, with tireless worthy sermons, letters from the National Viewers and Listeners Association, moral crusades inside and outside Parliament, and attempts to preserve or revive values which at various times will be labelled 'Victorian' or 'old-fashioned' or even 'Christian'. Or, Caiaphas will get disillusioned. He will notice that most of us do not take any notice of what he says, and he will conclude (because he thinks redemption is the same as improvement) that the majority of the human race is irredeemable. I am sorry to say that most great Christian thinkers have been of this mind – St Augustine, St Thomas Aquinas, Calvin and Pascal were all doubtful about the chances most of us have of getting to heaven. Dr Pusey was certain that most people would go to hell. Nowadays, of course, Caiaphas might not actually believe in hell, or indeed in religion. But the hallmark of his belief – that people should be cast away because they cannot be made better – is a fairly familiar note sounded nowadays in political, journalistic or even in medical circles. There was that paradoxical doctor who would not treat patients who smoked, and who put one in mind of the saying that they who are whole have no need of the physician, but they who are sick.

We who are sick, among whom I cheerfully number myself, cannot find in Caiaphas a very inspiring figure, even though we know that he and his like have governed and will always run the world, and the religions of the world. But among those who follow these religions there will always appear from time to time surprising characters who help us see the figure of Caiaphas' silent and devastating adversary. They are found in the most unlikely places. You would have thought that a medieval anchoress, walled up in a room on the edge of a little church in Norwich at the close of the fourteenth century, would be an obvious devotee of Caiaphas, living by rule, and denying within herself all that was life-enhancing and refreshing and true. And, indeed, in some passages of her visions, called the *Revelations of Divine Love*, we find not love, but a mere parroting of the more repugnant features of medieval piety.

But by the end of the visions, we realize that this anchoress,

Lady Julian, is one of the great Christian originals, who has illuminated Jesus for us in a way that few have done before or since.

In her most famous line, popularized by T. S. Eliot, she says that sin is behovely, or necessary. The Christian life is one of 'glad penitence'. 'In heaven we shall really and eternally see that we sinned grievously in this life: yet despite all this, we shall see that it made no difference at all to his love, that we are no less precious in his sight . . . For just as God by his courtesy forgives our sin when we repent, so he wills that we forgive our sin too' . . . 'God loves mankind' . . . 'who is and who will be sinful to the very end' . . . 'He loves us eternally and we sin constantly!'

Lady Julian does not attempt to deny human sinfulness. Nor can anyone read her positively ghoulish meditations on the passion and the wounds of Christ and suppose that she thought that sin did not really matter, or that it did not have its price. She believed it to have a price, the only price which, according to Christian orthodoxy, could be exacted. Yet there have been few minds in history (except perhaps William Blake's) which we feel further from pharisaism.

It is always open to us to spurn whatever gifts appear, either by grace or luck, in our path. Nobody will force us to live adventurously. We can bury our talent in the ground. We can turn away from Jesus sorrowfully – for we possess too much. We can play life by the rules, and die a little each day as we do so. After a time, even we will stop noticing. The nice thing about emotional and moral atrophy is that it works as its own anaesthetic, and even, as in the case of the Pharisee in the temple, it can dress itself up as virtue.

Or we can live in a different way. The preparedness to make mistakes, and an openness to the possibility of being hurt are signs of life; where life is, for a Christian, love will be, and where love is, life will be. 'Owe no man anything but to love one another, for he that loveth another hath fulfilled the law' (Romans 13:8). Caiaphas longs for us to say that it is all much more complicated than that, because to leave it at that is such a risky business. Where does it leave the vast areas of canon law, liturgy, or the traditions of Christian spirituality, if you simply tell people to live their lives and risk loving, because God loves them? Shouldn't the Church be taking some kind of lead – I mean about the collapse of contemporary morality; where do we stand on the various methods of contraception now available, or on the vitally important issue of inter-church relations, or the most important issue of all in the entire universe, the ordination of women to the priesthood? Surely we need guidelines on these things, and the churches should be helping us to make up our minds? Why does not the Church speak out more firmly about AIDS; and this revolting film they have now released about Jesus, shouldn't that be stopped; and why are the bishops so utterly feeble either in attacking or in not attacking the Government?

Lady Julian has an answer for these questioners. She waited fifteen years after her visions had disappeared before the last word came to her:

> You would know our Lord's meaning in this thing? Know it well. Love was his meaning. Who showed it you? Love. What did he show you? Love. Why did he show it? For love. Hold on to this and you will know and understand love more and more. But you will not know or learn anything else – ever!

# 'Person' and Risk (2)*

## Elizabeth Templeton

*Theologian*

'An honest religious thinker', wrote the philosopher Wittgenstein in 1948, 'is like a tightrope walker. He almost looks as though he were walking on nothing but air. His support is the slenderest imaginable. And yet it really is possible to walk on it.'

In a sense, my agenda for this essay is to reflect on the tightrope walking which is quite normal for us when we love one another, bring up children, remake the world in paint or drama, explore the sub-atomic world or the galaxies, and generally do most of the things associated with being alive rather than dead. That agenda was offered to me under the sub-heading: 'The *individual* and risk', but since I can no longer use the word 'individual' except in a sinister sense which I hope to clarify, I redefine my task as being some exploration of what is risky about being a person, and what bearing that has on theology.

One of my friends would, if she either really believed in God, or was quite sure that he did not exist, be tempted to kill herself tomorrow. That is to say, if she thought that around the nightmare which her life has largely been, there was ultimate safety, love and acceptance: or if she could know that there was nothing, she would not live longer with the constant wounding which being alive in the world is to her. At the worst times, all that blocks her desire to take herself out of it is the risk that the God of her childhood, the creator and sustainer of hell, might then produce for her an endless environment for which this ghastly world was merely a premonitory trial run.

Such a sense of cosmic risk may not be typical of the well-enough mothered and fathered child, but let it stand as one pole, the negative one, of the *menace* theology can bear to humankind.

For those believers who find risk a more bearable theme, the tone of risk-taking is more positive, as most of the chapters in this book have suggested – risk, for instance, as participation in the risk-taking of God involved in creating a free and complex world, risk as entering the vulnerability of Jesus, risk as moral courage, risk as the mode of our tempering to the resilience and elasticity of those who are to be made fit for unlimited caviare and trumpets.

Between these poles of the angels and the wild beasts, of hopeful and threatening risk, which is creative and which is destructive risk-taking? Are we in the end justified in taking the kind of risk involved in believing in God at all in such a world as this? What counts, anyway, as *justifying* risk-taking? Is it a good outcome, the mere fact that in the end the risk was worth it, or was not so great as it seemed? Is it the prudence of the calculation on the outcome, whether or not it is probably a 'safe' risk? Or is it the wholeheartedness of the investment we have in the outcome, whatever the probabilities? When does moral courage lurch into feckless bravado? When is risk-taking 'hubris', the overstepping of human and cosmic limits which provokes the wrath of God? And when is it responsible? Does it make a difference if the risk is for the sake of others, or simply for the hell, or the heaven, of it?

So many questions can ricochet off the essays in this book; and I am sure that if we had delicate enough instruments to sound any company of believers and sceptics, we would find that people differ immensely, not only about what risks seem to them actually involved in believing and not believing, but also about their answers to these secondary questions. One man's outward-bound course is another man's hell. There would be temperamental and political variables as to risk-tolerance, linked perhaps to the different levels of anxiety, impatience, corruption, zest and security which clearly condition people's theological responses to anything.

My intention, however, is to shoot the rapids of these turbulent psycho-sociological waters, not to swim in them. For I am persuaded that whatever the conditioning of our responses, the connection between personhood and risk is not, for human beings, accidental or deplorable, though often terrifying.

Most people, I imagine, have at least tasted what the psychiatrist-God of T. S. Eliot's *The Cocktail Party* says to one protagonist:

> Let me tell you, that to approach the stranger
> Is to invite the unexpected, release a new force,
> Or let the genie out of the bottle.
> It is to start a train of events
> Beyond your control.

Much of that play is about the elusiveness of people to one another, even in the supposed intimacy of marriage. But its dramatic climax is bound up with the fate of a young woman, Celia Coplestone, who so craves for something she cannot find in the brittle familiarity of the cocktail party that she goes off into the real strangeness of a *via dolorosa* which ends in her death. The journey is to be terrible, and at one point the psychiatrist himself is wavering about whether Celia can cope with it, only to be answered by another of the play's 'cosmic guardians':

> She will be afraid of nothing; she will not even know
> That there is anything there to be afraid of.
> She is too humble. She will pass between the scolding hills,
> Through the valley of derision, like a child sent on an errand,
> In eagerness and patience. Yet she must suffer.

Adults, of course, and parents in particular, are those who are aware of the dangers (and normally feel superior about it). But it should perhaps be a question to our self-esteem that children (and saints?) take risks, are at risk, quite unselfconsciously. Do we pay enough attention to 'innocence' in the theological exploration of risk?

If not, it is probably because we take it as axiomatic that most of us, men and women under the sun, are incapable of such innocence, especially if we inhabit the late twentieth century, and have, to boot, read through a collection of essays on 'theology and risk'. We publicly acknowledge, or at least privately suspect, that even if we have learned to walk the tightrope of faith as if the solid concrete of the Forth Road Bridge were spread beneath our feet, there is all around us hostile air, into which we may at any moment find ourselves hurtling.

In spite of that, it seems to me that even twentieth-century Christians, jittery as they often are about doctrine, psychology, politics, and so on, share with the rest of the world a common human experience of the strangeness of themselves to themselves, as the future, the other, is engaged with. Our capacity for that engagement is, I believe, what makes the hair even on our responsible, careful, fallen adult necks still prickle with recognition at what I take as my central theological text for this essay. That text is the opening line of a poem by e. e. cummings: 'love's function is to fabricate unknownness.'

Most people who hear British news bulletins, or stagger through the normal ups and downs of any human week, know that big and small newnesses lurk round every corner, and have to be faced. The unplanned child is conceived. The planned child is hit by a bus. You win the pools. The mother finds a breast lump. A new job is offered. The man falls in love with another woman. The brie turns out to be poisoned. More or less at first hand, most of us have to cope with *bearing* such things.

But 'love's function is to *fabricate* unknownness'?! Not to sustain it, like a punch on the chin, but to generate it, to be its very source. What does this mean?

My main contention for the rest of this chapter is that there is a *kind* of agnosticism, a proper response to the hiddenness of ourselves, of one another and of God, which is not the *frustration* of our knowing any of them, but the *manifestation* of it. Now is that proper or improper risk?

To state the case, I need to be forgiven a historical excursion, apparently remote from my agenda, but now for me bound up with all the questions as to who we are, who we really are, what the risks are that we are not who we think we are. I need also to be forgiven the sketchiness of a hit-and-run handling of the issues.

Whatever you make, or don't make, of the Christian doctrine

of the Trinity, it seems to me to have set new standards for
the intertwinedness of what it is to be a person: to be one
whose identity is constituted and defined in relationship: for
whom relating is not an option, because not to be related would
be not to be: and yet to be one whose identity is not absorption
into some undifferentiated cosmic soup, since it is the irreplaceable particularity of each which generates the dynamism of
every other's being.

Since I first met it, I have been intellectually and emotionally
teased by a symbol which the Celtic Christians apparently took
over from an old pagan emblem for the interpenetration of air,
fire and water. I warn you, of course, if you need warning, to
beware of the theological health hazard of using geometry as
a key to metaphysics; but if you treat it as what Ian Ramsey
might have called a 'disclosure model', you may be at less risk
of being bewitched.

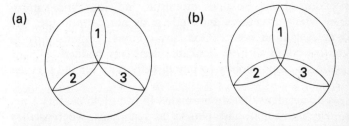

In the first picture, each segment is atomic: that is to say, it
can be detached from the other segments and survive intact,
with only its relative position altered. In the second, (the grave-
stone symbol in question) each segment is so involved with the
others that if any segment were to be removed, the other two
would be thereby dismantled, left gapingly without structure.
The identity of any one depends on the mutual involvement of
all three.

This, of course, does not *prove* anything. (The works of
Martin Escher demonstrate how drawable the impossible is.) I
find it, however, suggestive of two real alternatives, two direc-
tions of being and knowing which are actually livable and lived.
I call the difference between them the difference between being
an 'individual' and being a 'person'.

Western Europe has taken over from classical Aristotelian philosophy a massive and significant tradition of thinking which tends to equate 'being' and 'being intelligible'. To *be* is to be knowable: and to *know* is to be able to categorize and to classify, to have things taped by species and genus, to master them by having their identification under control. A thing is itself and not another thing. This produced a model of the world as legions of things existing in themselves due to the causality of a Prime Mover, and of ourselves as observing, rational, animated and social registrars of what was there.

This understanding of being and knowing was given Christian baptism by St Augustine, who also dramatized our quest for the knowledge of God as being played out ultimately in the responsible intactness of each embattled soul. Over the sixteen hundred odd years since then, by way of Aquinas and Calvin, by Reformation leaps and Romantic bounds, Western Europe has endorsed the isolated, atomistic, individualistic anthropology which structures and undergirds our cultural life. Me and my salvation before God: my criminal responsibility in court: my room with the lockable door: my padded cell: my Thatcherite responsibility to pay directly only for the services I use.

It is no accident that we normally, in twentieth-century English, use 'individual' and 'person' as synonyms, whereas they seem to me to be at anthropological war with one another. For it is a matter of culture and not of inevitability that we make them synonyms. Of course, we are all to some extent the prisoners of our separating skins, but there are *better* cultures. (One of my etymological pleasures is the knowledge that Peter Berger's book title *The Homeless Mind* can only be translated in a certain African language by a phrase best retranslated: 'The one who is far away from where he belongs'.)

It has taken in the West the Kantian revolution in philosophy, the rise of Existentialism and the sociology of knowledge to retrieve at all the interpenetration of us and what we know; and that has galloped off, heaven help us, towards Idealist and Constructivist sunsets. And, on the whole, we are as a culture twitchy and apologetic about self-involving knowledge, as if it were a deviation from proper, objective, neutral, detached, impersonal, accuracy-bearing inspection of things.

e. e. cummings' line, if taken seriously, crystallizes quite another way of looking at being and knowing, which is much more important in Semitic and Byzantine imagination. (One can hardly say in Semitic theory, because the characteristic mode of their exploration was narrative.) Knowing *is* loving. Being known *is* being loved, not a preliminary to or a consequence of it. Knowledge is therefore a passionate act, a drowning. Naming is cherishing, cradling, stewarding, being so bound up with the other that the being of one is at stake when the other is at risk. Being something, being someone is not an intact state, but a movement-towards, an exchange, an ecstasy.

Of course, even in an entrenchedly atomistic culture, rumours of angels happen. Ecstasy will out; and bruising. But it is harder for them to make intelligent sense of themselves, to present themselves as more than a bubble-bath of subjectivity in which we recover from our serious cognitive enterprises. 'Knowing' and 'feeling' split off, the latter relegated to the private, inner world, or, in the counter-culture of some, elevated as *better* than knowing, a substitute for futile arguments about truth.

This may all seem a very long way from the stated agenda of reflection on specific human activities like parenting, doing art or science or politics. But in a way these merely seem to me areas in which we test and manifest the polarities of our existence between living as individuals and living as persons. Unless that distinction meets some recognition the rest of this chapter will be, as perhaps it has already been, unintelligible.

Being childed is to me a more significant theological experience than parenting, if you see what I mean. For children are natively persons – which is why I think they were spotlighted as evangelical exemplars.

As a supposedly active parent, I am much of the time on a kind of *via negativa*, discovering what it is like *not* to be God – in those characteristic family scenarios where protective instinct and the recognition of freedom clash; where the desire for socialization and control makes it tempting to manipulate and direct and even design in advance the shape of another life; where dilemmas generated by finite time, space and energy bombard one into fragmented responses to whole people. (None of this is unique to the relationship of parenting, of course: it's just very crudely clear at twenty to nine in the morning as you struggle to get X's teeth brushed while Y is weeping in desolation because the dinosaurs are all dead.)

On the other hand, one of the amazements of parenting is being constantly 'godded' by the challenge of this awful purity of desire, rage, love and hate which belongs to children, and which threatens the stabilities of social convention and habituated prudence. 'Godded', too, in the forgiveness of sins, as a small child offers you yourself in the waking of each morning with no holding of warranted grudges, not even with magnanimous withholding of reproach for the snarls of yesterday, but with forgetfulness – though, developmentally, memory is possible – forgetfulness of everything except the expectation that you are there to get on with being mother and father. I find it interesting that in all our cultural struggles about motherhood and fatherhood in God, no one has, to my knowledge, done a serious, unsentimental theology of childhood. Have we really failed to notice, or are we frightened of this paradigm of personhood in common life, robustly resistant to collectivism, absorption and neglect, and yet unbolstered by any myth of self-sufficiency?

The main risk of parenting, it seems to me, or of adulting, is that we evade, deflect or suppress that challenge, that we unconfessingly, even proudly, reconcile our children to the normal fallenness of things, the 'proper' limits of responsibility, property, community. All my children, in the first year of school, have come home wearing well-intentioned anti-molester badges with the legend: 'Say no to the stranger' – children who instinctively rebuke me and are ashamed of me when I have avoided or refused beggars or derelicts on city streets.

It is relatively obvious to apply this person/individual distinction to the realm of inter-human relations, whether domestic or political, but much harder to extend it to the cosmos, for most of us the realm of given, 'out-there' objectivity.

That is why the second unwritten book I want to read after a theology of childhood is a theology of art – though Nicholas Berdyaev and Martin Buber have both been immensely suggestive here. For the artist, in whatever medium, be it words, paint, sound, celluloid, does to the stuff of the world what we at best do to one another – wrestles with it in a way which takes us further into the newness, the unknownness of what is there; and is made and dismantled in the process. Of course, the ostensible human being – Picasso, Rembrandt, Bergman, Epstein, Beethoven – is there, a body in the co-ordinates of space and time. But what actually *identifies* them, creatively speaking, is the particular, irreplaceable way they deal with light, shape, sound waves, bronze. In that action, what Buber calls the sacrifice and risk of addressing the world and being addressed with the primary word 'I – Thou', the artist becomes himself, and new worlds, re-presented worlds, unknown worlds are articulated against the gravity pull of what is merely the case. (There are of course other theories of art, as mirror, as self-expression, as construct, but I suspect they trivialize the mutuality and agnosticism of the creative engagement, where, so to speak, neither world nor maker knows what will become of them till they are made.)

To speak of science, as I was also bidden, would really be bad faith on my part, since my encounter with what scientists are about is desperately second-hand. I share an impression, which David Jenkins has suggested earlier in this book, that science is becoming more open and tentative and fluid about reality than it would have been in the heyday of its grip on the British mind. The language of detachment, isolation, absolute certainty, public consensus is, at least in some circles, giving way to a recognition of scientific activity as imaginative, risk-taking, relative to those who do it and trust-involving. That, I am sure, needs to be pursued. But I feel a little like the report some years ago in the *Church Times*, where an account of an open debate at a British Council of Churches Assembly between Tom Torrance and Ian Ramsey on theology and science ended with the words: 'At this point, the press bench was unable to follow the argument.'

At any rate, I suspect that in whatever field of human engagement with reality, the struggle to say what is true, and our irreplaceable commitments and alignments in engaging with reality are inextricable. That is why we need one another to have a hope in hell of knowing anything. I would love theology to be the depth-articulation of that, to put into words and enactment, with intelligent seriousness, how an epistemology of love and relatedness clarifies what actually goes on in the world. But whether, in public culture, we can get theology out of the kennel where it has been deservedly tied up for aridity, pietism and intellectual sluggishness remains to be seen.

This takes me into the last question on my remit. What is the relation of all this exploration of risk to traditional theological doctrine? Is traditional faith itself at risk? And, if so, are we all menacedly at sea?

In my lecturing days, if I had put a question in an exam which included the phrase 'traditional theological doctrine', it would have been with malice aforethought, to sort out the men from the boys. For I would have expected the bad students to think they knew what the phrase meant, and the good students to know that they didn't. That is, I can only use the phrase ironically, or with inverted commas. The more you specify times and places, of course, the easier it may be to approximate to content; for instance, the doctrine of John's Gospel, or of Nicene Orthodoxy, or of twelfth-century Rome, or of the Calvinist Reformation (though even each of these, in all conscience, exhausts battalions of wrestling scholars). But if you think there is one detectable, identical, steady-state body of dogma, unaltered at all times and places, you need a theologian other than me to service your reflections. If we are in the business of articulating a theology which does justice to the risky openness of personhood, tradition is not 'back there', but in the futurity of our unfinished conversation and communion with the past. It's a bit like Norman Nicholson's image of perfection:

Perfection is not the land you leave
It is the pole you measure from: it gives
Geography to your ways and wanderings.

Taking more on trust than my Greek and my reading-time

allow, I believe that at various points, Christian theology has actually suggested as much to the world, and that all creative liturgy is nerved by such an understanding. But, of course, the Adamic theologian in all of us prefers to bite off apples he can competently chew, instead of wrestling with the unnamed God for our knowledge of good and evil.

When I was a university student in Glasgow, some twenty years ago, I used to go home on the subway in the pre-smartened days when the trains rattled and creaked their way beneath the Clyde, full of spit and cigarette ends. One day, across from me on the lurching seat were four assorted denizens of the city of culture. There was a battered old housewife, headscarfed and splay-shoed, clutching a worn shopping bag – what the patois would call 'an old bauchle'. There was a stolid workman in grimy dungarees under a navy donkey-jacket, and there were two vacant-eyed youths in studded leather and jeans. They shoogled monotonously as the terminus of my visual field, as people did every day, and I was paying no attention to them. Suddenly, I noticed, sticking out of the lower pocket of the donkey-jacket, the head and shoulders of a small doll.

Quite what then happened is hard to describe. It was neither speculating nor imagining: but I suddenly *saw* these four people rivetingly beautiful, not changed in shape or clothes or position, but suddenly hallowed and clean, as if all the dust and stupidity had been sloughed off. Then, after a moment, the four were reabsorbed into the everydayness of the train, and I started wondering who the doll was for.

Now of course, the episode *proves* nothing, and I hesitate even to tempt the spiritual voyeurism of a theologically starved culture by telling it. But as I struggled with my brief for this essay, it kept jumping into my head as a quickening, a parable of what I am trying to say about our quite mundane experiences of love-knowing another person, or love-knowing the fragile earth. All that was odd about it was that it happened out of the blue, with quite anonymous people. But that very strangeness is what makes me risk receiving it as theologically and politically suggestive gift, rather than as freak, delusion or incipient psychosis. For what else should be expected, if the ground of our unknownness is a God for whom there are no strangers?